ICH DIEN

TIPPEE & TWADDLE.
Pub.d as the Act directs by J. Carter, Oxford Street Nov 27. 1786.

# GEORGE IV
## A LIFE IN CARICATURE

KENNETH BAKER

With 211 illustrations

Thames & Hudson

*To our grandchildren – Tess, Conrad, Oonagh, Evie and Fraser*

Half-title **Tippee and Twaddle**
27 May 1786
WILLIAM DENT

*The two broomsticks, which were symbols of the married state, clearly show
that George and Maria were man and wife. 'Tippee' and 'Twaddle' were slang
recommended by George Hanger – the word 'twaddle' first appeared in 1782.*

Frontispiece **A Voluptuary Under the Horrors of Digestion** (detail)
2 July 1792
JAMES GILLRAY

*George was just 30 years old when Gillray drew this famous image. The
slim figure has given way to the bursting waistcoat; the glutton has almost
finished a ham; the empty bottles are under the table; the chamber pot is
ready behind the chair; the books of gambling debts are on the floor; and the
cures for the pox are on the table. George had been unable to resist succumbing
to temptation – the die was cast. He could never say no – his French chef,
Carême, said some 16 years later, 'Your Highness, my concern is to tempt
your appetite – not to curb it.'*

Opposite **A Peep into the Punch Room at the Pavilion, or, The Gouty Adonis!**
GEORGE CRUIKSHANK

p. 7 **Portrait of the Prince Regent, later George IV, in his Garter Robes**
(detail)
1816
THOMAS LAWRENCE

First published in the United Kingdom in 2005 by
Thames & Hudson Ltd, 181A High Holborn, London WC1V 7QX

www.thamesandhudson.com

© 2005 Kenneth Baker

British Library Cataloguing-in-Publication Data
A catalogue record for this book is available from the British Library

ISBN-13: 978-0-500-25127-0
ISBN-10: 0-500-25127-4

Printed and bound in China by C & C Offset Printing Co. Limited

**A note on price conversions**

The Office of National Statistics provides a consumer price inflation list
going back to medieval times. The inflation index for 2003 is 715.2.
This means an amount in 1780, for example, has to be multiplied by 715.2
and then divided by 6.3, the index for 1780. The ONS table tends to give
slightly higher amounts than previous conversion tables.

# CONTENTS

# PREFACE

I STARTED TO COLLECT 18th- and 19th-century political caricatures over forty years ago. At that time you could pick them up from small antiques shops and market stalls for a few pounds – the most I ever paid for a large Gillray was £40. I was fascinated by them, as they told a political story involving some figures that I recognized – George III, George IV, Pitt, Fox, Burke and Wellington – but to find out what was happening in each print was a challenge for historical detection. (I had not yet come across the superb catalogue of the British Museum's print collection, which was compiled by Dorothy George in the middle of the last century.)

Political caricature was 'invented' in London in the 1730s. Its golden age, from 1780 to 1830, was dominated by its star genius Gillray, but there were many other engravers – Rowlandson, Dent, Sayers, Newton, Isaac, George and Robert Cruikshank, Woodward, William and Henry Heath, Seymour and Doyle. Their prints were engraved, printed and coloured overnight to provide material for the flourishing trade of the print shops, which sold these prints over the counter for one shilling plain and two shillings coloured.

I have always wanted to widen the appreciation of these prints, to bring them to a larger audience. They tell a fascinating story about our past and they bring to life events and personalities in a way that no prose narrative can. So one of my purposes is to engage the attention, particularly of younger people, and spark an interest in all those events that have helped to shape the society in which we live today. To acquire knowledge through amusement and laughter makes the study of the past easier, more interesting and more approachable.

Most of the prints in this book are from my own collection but I have included some from national collections.

I would like to thank Antony Griffiths, Keeper of the Department of Prints and Drawings at the British Museum; David Beevers, Keeper of Fine Art at the Royal Pavilion, Libraries & Museums; Sara W. Duke, Associate Director, Prints and Photographs Division, Library of Congress; Jean-Robert Durbin of the Huntington Library, California; and the National Archives Image Library for their help in identifying and supplying prints.

I would also like to thank John Wardroper, a fellow enthusiast and historian, for proof-reading my book, and Kathy Fogarty, my secretary, without whom this book could not have appeared.

## The Game Cock and the Dunghills

22 April 1827

WILLIAM HEATH

*This celebrates the popularity of George's decision to appoint Canning as Prime Minister – the Cock of the Walk. The Tories who refused to serve are led by Wellington – Apostasy – saying 'Damne! I'm off' and Eldon – Hypocricy – dropping the Lord Chancellor's mace. John Bull, as a yokel, approves George's choice saying the Old Tory Guard had ruined the country and lined their own pockets. The Times said it was the battle of the throne versus the oligarchy.*

at each transient arrangement before it is all turned out for some other.'

J. H. Plumb, one of the greatest historians of the Hanoverians, appreciated the dilemma of contrasts that constituted George's life. 'Few kings have been so hated or so mocked or had their virtues so consistently ignored. For George IV possessed virtues. It was his sincerity which brought him into such scrapes and, what so many forget, regal self-indulgence, particularly in building and in the decorative arts, is almost always to the public advantage.'

George had an appetite for life and being the heir to the throne he was determined to enjoy it to the full. The weakness in his character was not that he was full of guile but that he was prone to be naïve and impulsive. He was open-hearted and surrendered his affections readily and passionately with scant regard for the consequences. His emotions were close to the surface: there are countless records of him weeping in public at

the news of some great misfortune or the death of one of his long-cherished friends. Denied any involvement in affairs of state by his father, he applied his energy to other things – some were trivial and transient, others more permanent. He had one great gift, which could only be described by the word 'gusto'; as Palmerston said in 1811, 'We are all at the kick and go.'

As a young man George had many affairs, including an illegal 'marriage' to Maria Fitzherbert, but he made the devastating mistake of allowing others, principally his father, George III, to choose his wife. Once married he soon found out that Caroline of Brunswick was a vulgar, uncultivated hoyden and within a matter of weeks he came to loathe her. She responded by belittling him, assuaging her rampant sexuality with a series of lovers. One of the footmen at her house in Blackheath, giving evidence to the Commission that was set up to examine her behaviour, said that 'The Princess loves fucking.' It is amazing that with his broad experience of women he consented to marry

Caroline. Max Beerbohm described her perfectly: 'She was the very embodiment of vulgarity: hard, implacable, German vulgarity.'

George spent the better part of twenty-five years trying to disentangle himself from this marriage, and his insistence upon a divorce, after Caroline had decided to return and claim a share to the throne, led to a series of events that made him the subject of huge derision. One can sympathize with his intention to exclude Caroline, but his methods were politically and personally disastrous: when she returned to England she was the people's Queen. Within nine months of the evidence of her conduct having been revealed they turned against her, finding that George's opinion of her was not far off the mark – but the damage had been done.

What I have done in this biography is to use the caricatures of the time to tell the story of George's life as it was seen by his contemporaries. He had the great misfortune to live right through the golden age of English caricature from 1780 to 1830 when the high and the mighty were not spared, and so many of these caricatures are irreverent. Caricature originated in 16th-century Italy and the word 'caricatura' from which caricature is derived means 'load or charge' possibly as a firearm. It exaggerates particular physical characteristics, the clothes and habits of its victims in order to expose the true aspects of their character in a way no official portrait could. Caricature was sometimes propaganda for a cause and several of the caricaturists of the late 18th century were imbued with a moral fervour, striking down the powerful and pompous with their most powerful weapon – humour. It was possible to censure plays or to put up the price of newspapers – 'twopenny trash' – thereby placing them beyond the reach of working men, but it was virtually impossible to prosecute a joke. Although George III, George IV, Pitt and Fox all would have loved to suppress certain caricatures, as others did in the more authoritarian culture of France, they were not able to stop them in more liberal England. It was a blessing in disguise, for if a people can laugh at their rulers they don't find it necessary to cut off their heads. The target was not the overthrow of the monarchy but a reform of the Parliamentary system and the corruption that supported it, and for that they focused on the prodigal son and his ministers.

The caricaturists of that age were like the paparazzi of today. Instead of a photo-lens they used their etching needles to cut images onto copperplates to capture the events of the day. The political and social centre of London was quite small, stretching from Westminster to Charing Cross, the City and back to St James's, Piccadilly, Green Park and Buckingham House, which meant that the artists could quite easily see the major figures in their grand houses, in the galleries of the House of Commons and House of Lords, and as they went riding in the parks. Gillray lived above the print shop of Hannah Humphrey, at number 27 on St James's Street, which was the very centre of the political world. On one side was Brooks's Club where the Whigs went to carouse, gamble, plot and dream of power. Opposite was White's where the Tories went to carouse, gamble, plot and enjoy the fruits of office. Gillray just had to step down from his attic bedroom to see all the political figures of the day, carrying with him his pencil and a small card, 1.5 inches by 3 inches, to capture the likeness that he would later distort.

Many daily papers circulated in the coffee houses – *The Times,* the *Morning Chronicle,* the *Evening Star* – and they carried the gossip of the Court, London society, and Parliament that provided substance for the caricaturists, who had to work very quickly to capture the fleeting moment. Plates would be engraved overnight, inked, and a number of copies run off on the printing presses – the first being coloured by the artist and then copied by a roomful of girls. The next morning the prints were put up in the windows of the print shops to be sold to the passer-by for 'a shilling plain' and 'two shillings coloured'. This was the first time that many of the ordinary inhabitants of London could see and recognize the people set in authority over them.

The print-shop trade was very vigorous and demanded a continuous supply of prints. Beside Hannah Humphrey at 27 St James's Street, there were William Fores at the corner of Sackville Street in Piccadilly; Ackermann, a German builder of carriages, in the Strand where he established a fine print business concentrating on topographical themes; and clustered around St Paul's were several dealers selling to bankers and clerks, the most important dealer being Thomas Tegg. At times large crowds would gather outside the print shops eager to see the latest satire and to have a good laugh.

The victims would have much preferred to be depicted as noble statesmen, but it was not to be – Pitt was an emaciated drunkard, Fox was a swarthy, unkempt and dangerous revolutionary, George III a bumbling farmer, and the Prince of Wales a profligate voluptuary. Many of the cartoons in this book do not aim to flatter and few evoke an instinctive sympathy, but they tell a story which is not always to the detriment of George, the Prince of Wales, George the Regent, or George the King. The early ones, from 1780 to 1812, confirm how difficult it was for him to fill the role of the Prince of Wales, a lesson later learnt by Edward VII, Edward VIII and Prince Charles. To be a prince appears to be one of the most glittering strokes of good fortune and to be born the Prince of Wales should be the very best silver spoon. In reality that has rarely proved to be the case. The lives of princes are often a melancholy trail beset by isolation and indulgence, accompanied by envy, softened by flattery, undermined by ambition, and threatened by usurpation. They are so prominent that many who come into their presence, even for a short time, rush to record the fact in their diary or memoirs with tantalizing details, and their personal servants, familiar with all their foibles, their mistresses and cronies, are generators of gossip, and a source of malicious stories, which even in the 18th century the press was poised to buy. As the historian Edward Gibbon observed, 'In the private anecdotes of princes the lie is more easy as the detection is more difficult.'

The crescendo of ridicule reached its peak in 1820 during George's attempts to get a divorce, but quickly died away. For the rest of his reign George was treated more respectfully and during his state visits he drew some comfort from the fact that at least some of his subjects actually liked him. He mellowed, appeared less in public, corpulence took its toll, and he became for the last year of his life a virtual recluse at Windsor – it was a sad end. George was stranded by the march of intellect, by the transformation of a pastoral economy into an industrial one, by the growing high-mindedness of a society that wanted change; and by the growing resentment of the middle classes, who as taxpayers funded his foibles. But there was a certain grandeur about his declining years and he kept his dignity in seclusion, acquiring the appearance of a rather splendid ruin that had survived from another age. The satirists too had all but disappeared. George Cruikshank – the last of a great line – turned to the more lucrative business of book illustration: the politicians and the Court breathed a collective sigh of relief.

**The Slap Up Swell Wot Drives When Hever He Likes**

April 1829

WILLIAM HEATH

*A flattering portrait. The broad brimmed hat is regularly featured and in his later years George wore darker clothes as they helped to disguise his girth.*

# 1 The Party Boy

ON REACHING THE AGE OF EIGHTEEN in 1780 George was provided with his own establishment and, in the words of Horace Walpole, 'he began to make the greatest noise.' He moved in a very fast set and from 1781 onwards there were many reports in the London papers of drunken balls, gambling parties, brawls, and visits to the pleasure gardens of Vauxhall and the 'nunneries' in the vicinity of Pall Mall. There was also the possibility that he had fathered an illegitimate daughter with a Mrs Grace Elliott – though there were several other candidates for that honour. George had fallen in with a group of profligate young rakes who spent their time drinking and whoring. This satirical poem, *The Devil Divorced*, appeared when he was twenty-one – anyone could fill in the blanks:

> First on my list a man of rank appears,
> Far versed in wickedness above his years.
> The ——— of ———, if I can ought foretell,
> Will most assuredly come down to hell.
> Whenever vice or lewdness lead the way,
> With what officious zeal doth he obey!
> Him no ambition moves to seek renown;
> To be esteemed the *greatest buck* in town
> Appears to be his wish and sole delight.
> Full many times at twelve o'clock at night
> I've known him drunk, with half a dozen more,
> Kick up a row, break lamps, perhaps a door,
> And to conclude the night, to bilk his w—e.

Quite early on George had acquired a taste for older women which led him to have affairs with Lady Augusta Campbell, the daughter of the Fifth Duke of Argyll; Lady Melbourne, whose fourth child George Lamb, brother of the future Prime Minister, may have been the Prince's; the singer Elizabeth Billington; the Countess of Salisbury who rode to hounds and who was twelve years older than the Prince; and Georgiana, the wife of the Fifth Duke of Devonshire, who had several other lovers. In 1782 the Duchess described George, just after his twentieth birthday:

> The Prince of Wales is rather tall, has a figure which though striking is not perfect. He is inclined to be too fat and look too much like a woman in men's clothes….His face is very handsome and he is fond of dress to a tawdry degree. He is good natured and rather extravagant.

Here is an all too typical report of a night's roistering in April 1787. At a party given by Lady Hope the Prince arrived towards midnight 'pale as ashes, and glazed eyes set in his head, and in short almost stupefied'. The Duchess of Cumberland calmed him but when the guests went in to supper he consumed one and a half bottles of champagne. He 'posted himself in the doorway, flung his arms around the Duchess of Lancaster and kissed her with a great smack, threatened to pull Lord Galloway's wig off and knock out his false teeth.' His friends managed to get him out into a carriage.

By the middle of the 18th century the passion for gambling had taken hold in London society. White's, Boodle's and Almack's were the leading clubs. In 1778 the former manager of Almack's, William Brooks, founded a new club in St James's Street for twenty-seven rich dandies known as Macaronies, most of whom came from the great Whig families – Charles James Fox joined when he was just sixteen. This was the fast set and night after night huge sums of money changed hands.

There were several card games: *trente et quarante* – also known as *rouge et noir* – where 30 and 40 are respectively the winning and losing numbers; *quinze*, in which the winner tries to get fifteen points or as close as possible before going bust; and faro, pharo, or pharaoh, a game in which bets are placed on the order in which certain cards are dealt singly from the top of the pack. The 1780s saw a craze in pharaoh and *quinze*, with many banks being set up in private houses as well as clubs. The Prince of Wales was introduced to gambling by playing at the bank run by his uncle, the Duke of Cumberland. During this time Fox regularly took the bank at Brooks's, where thousands of guineas changed hands in a night, and he ran up huge debts, but when the bailiffs moved into his house in St James's, his friends held a whip-round raising £65,000 to pay off his creditors.

Hazard was a throw of the dice against a particular number between 5 and 9 which had been chosen by the caster, and several people could play at once. There was also piquet (a card game imported from France), backgammon and whist – the

**The Gamester
Bes–t, or, A New
Way to Win Money**

13 May 1784

WILLIAM DENT

This recalls a bet that Fox had made some years earlier at Brooks's – namely that he had not shat in his breeches. Gamesters, including the Prince, who is enjoying this enormously, were prepared to bet on anything. The alleged event is described in a footnote to a poem called The Gamblers:

> The adventure is recorded of Mr Charles Fox, by which, it is said, he recovered ten thousand pounds – a Sum he had lost the same night at the Hazard-table. Charles suddenly retires from the Company, and bribing a vile Livery for the decent purposes of fouling his breeches, returns in full perfume to the Knights of the Black-Table. Reynard, as might be expected, is immediately accused…Charles denies it with a laugh and turns it off by saying, 'Foxes, you know, are sometimes apt to smell.' The Knights positively charge him with having befouled himself. Charles affects to be angry, demurs, and hesitates a bett….They take him up, with different betts, to the amount of the sum he had just lost….Charles rings for John, of whom he enquires, 'John who ——— in my breeches?' 'I did, your Honour.'

> …To foul thy breeches, some vile Livery hire:-
> Perfumed, return:- the purchas'd Odour flies;
> Various th'imputed cause, the vain Surmise;
> Till pressing round thee, with malicious Wit
> Sagacious Jockeys swear the Prince –
> …Demur with diffidence and look the lye:
> Then hesitate a Bett…

**The Gamblers
As It Ought to Be**

9 June 1786

*A pair of prints that admonishes the Prince: one shows him gambling with Fox and being quite prepared to pledge his star (a sign of his princely authority), while the second tells George that he ought to be kicking the gamblers out – unheeded advice, for they were his boon companions.*

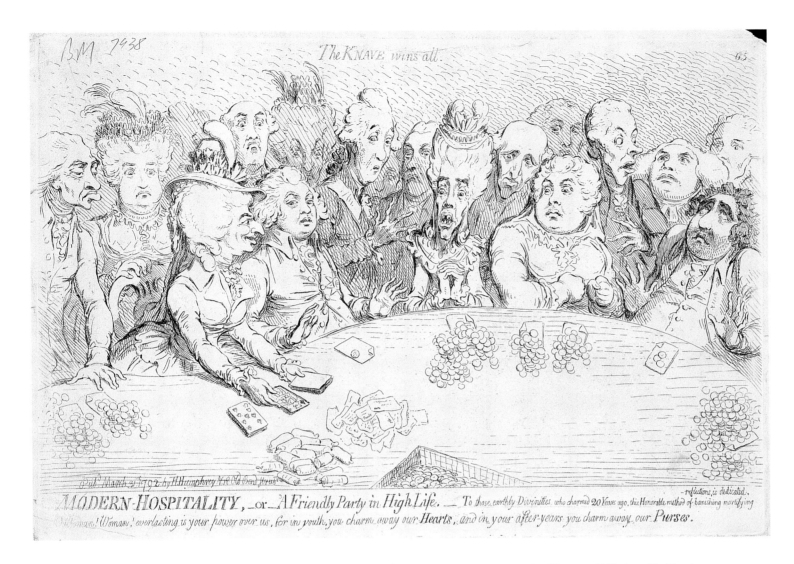

The KNAVE wins all.

MODERN-HOSPITALITY, _or _ A Friendly Party in High Life. _ To those earthly Divinities, who charmed 20 Years ago, this Honorable method of banishing mortifying

Pub. March 3.d 1792 by H.Humphrey N.18 Old Bond Street

– reflections, is dedicated.,

Woman! Woman! everlasting is your power over us, for in youth, you charm away our Hearts, and in your after-years, you charm away our Purses.

Duke of York's favourite, which he played for very high stakes (£5 a point and £25 on the rubber, £2,500 in today's money).

Fortunes vanished in a night's play and the moneylenders thrived – Howard and Gibbs, known as 'the Israelite establishment', were the most popular. Lord Lyttleton wrote, 'the rattling of a dice box at White's may one day or other shake down all our fine oaks.' Some, however, were lucky – Canning's father-in-law won £200,000 in one evening at White's playing whist: over £10 million at today's value.

In a typically casual way the aristocrats of Brooks's did not care who saw them gambling. The candles burned brightly in the windows, and as these windows were at ground level any passer-by could see the punters throwing away their fortunes.

## Modern Hospitality, or, A Friendly Party in High Life

31 March 1792

JAMES GILLRAY

*A faro party at Lady Archer's house – the party moved around London, rather similar to Nathan Detroit's floating crap game that had to move around Damon Runyon's New York. Hostesses included Lady Archer, here dealing the cards, and the very fat Mrs Hobart: both were the bankers and raked in the profits. It was alleged that George shared in the profits of Lady Archer's table.*

The ROYAL MINUET, or SAWBRIDGE'S DELIGHT.

*Pub<sup>d</sup> April 25 1788 by S. W. Fores N<sup>o</sup> 3. Piccadilly.*

## The Royal Minuet, or, Sawbridge's Delight

25 April 1788

JAMES GILLRAY

*At a party in Carlton House the Prince is spanking one of society's beauties, Mrs Sawbridge. He is surrounded by his usual crowd, Lady Archer and Maria Fitzherbert (to whom he was 'married' at the time), Fox and George Hanger – the Opposition at play. Several of the prints feature someone holding a whip – suggestive of more sophisticated pleasures.*

*Flagellation was a popular theme in late 18th-century erotica. Novellas with explicit titles were published –* Exhibition of Female Flagellants, *1777, and the intriguing* Lady Bumtickler's Revels. *In 1786 Gillray produced a print depicting Lady Termagent Flaybum preparing to birch her stepson.*

## A Hint for an Escape at the Next Spring Meeting

16 March 1792

ISAAC CRUIKSHANK

*George disposed of his stud in 1786 and started a new one in 1788. Within three years he had had 185 winners, including the Derby. At the Newmarket October meeting in 1791 his horse Escape, the favourite, was unexpectedly beaten although it was ridden by the champion jockey Samuel Chiffney. The following day Chiffney won on the same horse, which was for that race ranked as an outsider, and he was accused of pulling the first race to make a fortune on the second. After the Jockey Club banned Chiffney for his crime, the Prince of Wales put him on a pension of £200 until his death.*

## The Fall of Phaeton

1 July 1788

JAMES GILLRAY

*George was very proud of his horsemanship. Occasionally he drove his own carriage down to Brighton – on one occasion setting the record, there and back in ten hours. In 1788 he purchased four new 'cropt greys' for 400 guineas for his phaeton – the Ferrari of the day – which he liked to drive himself as he was an expert handler of horses. One evening in June the Prince's phaeton overturned in Kensington Gore and both he and Maria were thrown out. The Times reported that happily Maria had only sustained a 'swelling above the knee'. Within days three prints appeared showing either Maria's bare breast or bottom.*

The Fall of PHAETON.

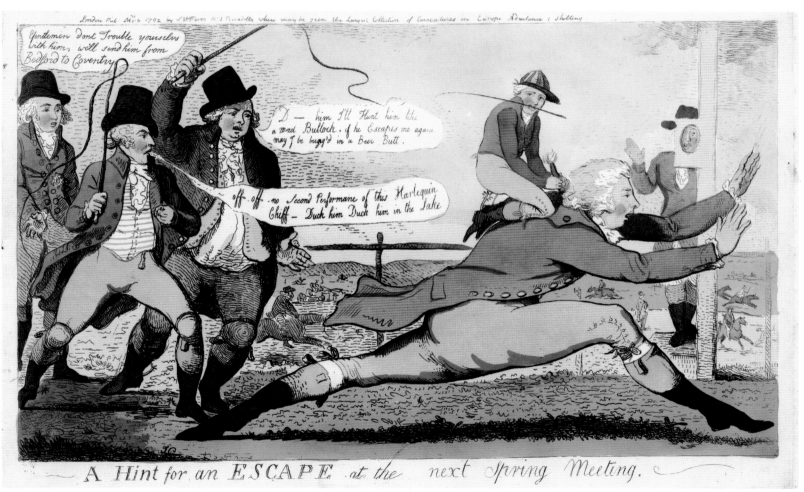

A Hint for an ESCAPE at the next Spring Meeting.

*The QUEENS.—*

*Pub.d April 17, 1787 by S.W. Fores at the Caracature Warehouse N.o 3 Piccadilly*

227

### The Queen's ——— [Ass]

17 April 1787

HENRY KINGSBURY (?)

*Queen Charlotte had been given a zebra, satirized as the Queen's Ass, and her favourite son reflects the striped splendour of the beast, which is featured in the picture behind him – without any doubt, a very smart man about town.*

### Frailties of Fashion

1 May 1793

ISAAC CRUIKSHANK

*Throughout his life George was a supporter of the fashion industry. It provided – as it does today – a great deal of employment. Here, as the leader of fashionable society, the Prince of Wales saunters through a park with Maria on one arm and the petite Duchess of York on the other. The print satirizes the fashion of the time for dresses to be padded at the front, which was useful to ladies who were pregnant – Maria's*

*FRAILTIES of FASHIO[N]*

dress is notably the most prominent. Two years earlier the fashion had been to have bustles at the back and a few years later the fashion was to change to straight, high-busted dresses. Fashion provided a lot of material for the printmakers and prints became the Vogue *and* Harper's Bazaar *of their day. As usual, France led but London was eager to follow.*

### Hint to Modern Sculptors, as an Ornament to a Future Square

3 May 1796

JAMES GILLRAY

*George was immensely proud of his appointment as Colonel of the Tenth Light Dragoons and he designed a new uniform for himself and his men: it was described as being 'very handsome but theatrical'. This print was copied as a signboard for a French inn.*

**The Dandy Taylor, Planning a New Hung[a]ry Dress**

15 May 1819

ISAAC CRUIKSHANK

George was infatuated with the uniforms of central and eastern Europe: he simply loved the buckles, belts, buttons, the epaulettes, all the furs, the frogging and the hats. Constantly redesigning the uniform of his beloved Tenth Regiment of Light Dragoon Guards, he looked upon them as a box of toy soldiers to be dressed in whatever took his fancy. He even ordered new uniforms on his deathbed. Here George is a tailor finding inspiration in three Hungarians.

George was fascinated by clothes, for he wanted to be the leader of fashionable society – and he spent a fortune to achieve that ambition. He rejected the extreme extravagances of the fops of the 1770s and 1780s, the Macaronies of Brooks's, with their pomaded perukes, their pinched, tight coats and pointed shoes. He set the fashion for simple, elegant lines: a style that Beau Brummell, another famous dandy of the era, also made very popular. Wigs disappeared, trousers replaced breeches, and in his later years George turned to the more subdued shades of brown and green.

In 1793 his unpaid tailors' bills amounted to £30,000. George would buy extravagantly – 74 pairs of gloves and 83 pairs of boots at a time. As his wife Caroline once remarked, 'He would have made an excellent tailor, or shoemaker, or hairdresser.' He also loved rings and bracelets and on some occasions wore so many that their sheer weight prevented him from signing official documents.

There was always an element of the actor in George and he loved to be the star of the show: on 4 June 1791 he appeared at Windsor for his father's birthday wearing a striped silk coat and breeches in claret-red and bottle-green, and a silver tissue waistcoat embroidered with silver thread and embellished with gems. Everything was covered with spangles and there were even diamond buttons on his coat and waistcoat. He also wore a 'diamond epaulette star, jewelled sword and buckles'.

### A View of the R–G—T's Bomb

August 1816

WILLIAMS

*Spain gave to the Prince Regent an enormous French mortar that had pounded Cadiz and was later abandoned by Soult after Salamanca. The bulbous nature of the bomb, which was pronounced 'bum', is mirrored by the Regent's bottom, barely disguised by the pointed red tails of his spencer coat. He has all the accoutrements of a dandy – a curled and powdered wig, a small pigtail, curled false whiskers, a crescent-shaped cocked hat, and two blue ribbons crossed over his corseted waist.*

A VIEW of the R d Ts BOMB.

**Our Fat Friend Going to Roost**

12 December 1820

JOHN MARSHALL

*George IV seeks consolation in three peeresses after the Divorce Bill has been dropped. He is totally plastered and they are putting him to bed – led by Lady Conyngham, who reassures him that she is as great as 'the Queen', meaning Caroline. The phrase 'Our Fat Friend' alludes to Beau Brummell's famous remark, 'Who's your fat friend?' Brummell was very lucky never to appear in any print.*

## A Real Brummagem Boy. The Man Wot Patronises the Button Makers

1830

*There was general industrial and agricultural distress in 1830, and Wellington was reported as being indifferent to the families' suffering – there were prints showing him surrounded by starving men and women. George alluded to these economic problems in a speech. Birmingham, a growing industrial centre, sent a deputation of journeymen button-makers to visit London and give a gift of gilt buttons to George. He helped them by making the buttons fashionable and setting a new trend. Many benefited from the 'dandyism' of George. On his death the trade of button-making was 'plunged into a desperate condition'.*

A REAL BRUMMAGEM BOY.

Published by G. Tregear, 123 Cheapside

THE MAN WOT PATRONISES THE BUTTON MAKERS.

Dean & Mundays Lithography. Threadneedle St

# 2 The Spendthrift

WHEN GEORGE III'S eldest son reached the age of twenty-one, the King granted him an annual income of £50,000 (£5 million in today's money) from the Civil List. The Prince, however, had expected to receive at least double that, as his father had received £100,000 when he came of age. This act of parental parsimony backfired, only intensifying George's resentment at his father's stinginess. He was also granted £60,000 to decorate and furnish Carlton House, but as far as George was concerned this was simply for starters.

By October 1784 George's Treasurer, Colonel Hotham, was advising the Prince 'that it is with grief and vexation that I now see your Royal Highness totally in the hands, and at the mercy, of your builder, your upholsterer, your jeweller, and your tailor'. The maintenance of his horses alone cost £30,000 a year, quite apart from other amounts that were owed – £32,777 to a coachmaker; £7,200 to a horse dealer; £34,000 to a variety of London tailors; and £947 to a Windsor apothecary for various medicines (no doubt some were to deal with venereal symptoms). His staff were not paid; tradesmen demanded payment when they recognized him in the street; and the workmen at Carlton House petitioned the Prime Minister for their wages. As a gesture of economy George temporarily closed Carlton House, sold a few horses and moved to Brighton; but he still found £54,000 to spend on jewelry for Mrs Fitzherbert.

In 1787 George and his brothers York and Clarence borrowed £350,000 (£35 million in today's money) from Jewish bankers in Holland, at an interest rate of five per cent. No repayment of the loan or interest was made and the bankers were

MONEY LENDERS

Pub.d Novem.r 8.t 1784 by W. Humphrey N.o 227 Strand

## Money Lenders

8 November 1784

THOMAS ROWLANDSON

*This is the first satire on the Prince's debts. Nonchalantly he sits at the table, stretching out his hand to two old Jewish moneylenders who have already affixed seals to his bond.*

THE BRIGHTON STUD

Pub.ᵈ JULY 30 1786 BY W. S. FORES AT THE CARACATURE WARE-HOUSE Nᵒ 3 PICCADILLY

## The Brighton Stud

3 July 1786

Another satire on the Prince's very public attempt at financial retrenchment: the Prince rides on an ass, which has the head of Maria Fitzherbert, accompanied by other asses including Hanger and Fox, and the whole procession is hissed at by geese. To cut his expenditure George had recently sold his stud at Tattersalls, the elite equine auctioneers.

The four corners of this print have been cut off because they had a strong glue on the back, which fixed them into a book. It was common practice in aristocratic households of the 18th century to collect prints and glue them to the pale-blue pages of large folios. Happily, this led to many prints being preserved in pristine condition.

33

## Return from Brighton, or, A Journey to Town for the Winter Season

23 October 1786

WILLIAM DENT

*After spending three months in Brighton, the Prince and Mrs Fitzherbert, holding a baby, rattle back to London with Fox and Sheridan whipping the horses on. The door of the carriage is decorated with a drawing of Maria depicted as Hope, holding an anchor topped with the Prince of Wales feathers.*

forced into bankruptcy. British bankers were expected to rally to the cause, but when Thomas Coutts lent the Prince £50,000 he made it clear that there was no more to come.

George's promises to put his house in order were like pie crusts – made to be broken. By 1790 his creditors were demanding a further £300,000. He was saved only by a generous loan from his French relative and drinking companion the Duc d'Orléans, who was the richest man in France. (George never had to repay this loan as Orléans was guillotined in 1793.) Just four years later, in 1794, Pitt was told that the Prince's debts were over £552,000 and the House of Commons refused to settle them. The only thing that could save the Prince would be to marry, at which Parliament agreed not only to pay off his debts, which soon rose to £639,890 (£53 million in today's money), but to increase his allowance to £100,000 a year.

RETURN FROM BRIGHTON,
OR A JOURNEY TO TOWN FOR THE WINTER SEASON.

NON COMMISSION Officers EMBARKING for BOTANY BAY

Published as the Act Directs Nov. 1st 1786 by H Humphrey Bond S.t & E Hedges N.º 92 Cornhill

**Non Comission Officers
Embarking for Botany Bay**

1 November 1786

JOHN BOYNE

In September the newspapers reported that the Government was
to send convicts, who could no longer be shipped to America, to
Botany Bay in Australia – an ideal destination for George and his
spendthrift friends. The Prince, astride a barrel of Imperial Tokay,
is wearing a fool's cap, happy to say goodbye to the moneylenders
and Maria Fitzherbert, and to set off for a new land with Hanger,
Fox, and Whigs Sheridan, Portland, North and Burke. They would
be free of their creditors.

The fiasco of the marriage simply increased the costs of the royal household. By 1803 £650,000 had to be written off and the Prime Minister insisted that in future there should be tighter controls on George's spending.

Throughout his life George spent what he wanted on whatever caught his fancy. Whim followed whim, and bill followed bill. He expected a grateful country to support him. But each administration grew less and less generous as the contrast between his frivolous, foppish frippery and the harsh reality of a country at war, deeply enmeshed in economic troubles, became greater and greater.

*The PRINCE at Grass.*

## The Prince at Grass; The Prince in Clover

2 June 1787

JAMES GILLRAY

*These two prints were published on the same day, just after Pitt had proposed to Parliament a settlement for the Prince's debts of £161,000 (in today's money over £15 million); a final payment for Carlton House of £20,000; and an increase of £10,000 out of the revenue of the Duchy of Cornwall. Prior to this Pitt and his ministers are shown pulling down the scaffolding outside Carlton House and driving away the unpaid artisans. Fox, North and Burke console the Prince and point to his rising sun. But everything comes right in the second print. Two Treasury Secretaries deliver the loot; Pitt is about to kiss the Prince's arse; and Fox and his friends rejoice, for Parliament has bailed out their friend.*

*LOVE'S Last SHIFT.*

## Love's Last Shift

26 February 1787

*Back from Brighton, London was no better. The conditions are squalid – Maria darns George's breeches while he rocks the cradle; the table is laid for one; Louis Weltje, controller of George's kitchen, unpacks potatoes; Hanger holds only a mug; and all they have to eat is a calf's head. The title is taken from Colley Cibber's first play,* Love's Last Shift, or, The Fool in Fashion.

*The PRINCE in Clover.*

## A Meeting of Creditors

3 April 1795

ISAAC CRUIKSHANK

*The Prince is surrounded by madams and courtesans, all presenting their accounts. The fat one with the gouty leg is selling the maidenhood of young virgins, one of whom stands behind her; the black woman on the left demands payment for other delights and carries on her waist a small birch rod. The woman next to the Prince lists on her bill 'My nose 20' – her nose has been eaten away by syphilis. This emphasizes how essential it was for George to get married and hold off the gangs of moneylenders, tradesmen, gamblers and bawds.*

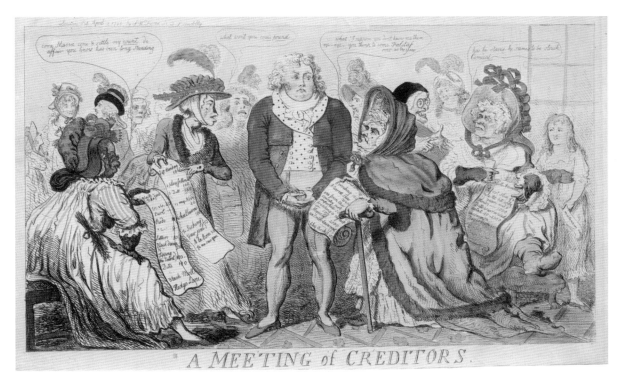

A MEETING of CREDITORS.

NO GRUMBLING

## No Grumbling

6 May 1795

ISAAC CRUIKSHANK

*George III, assisted by the Prince and Pitt, loads George's debts on to John Bull, who is almost bursting under the burden of taxes, some real and some imaginary. The small house is John Bull's barber shop – the Hair Powder Tax had come into force on 6 May and 'No Grumbling' was a catchphrase used in relation to the tax. The proposal to settle the Prince's debts had been tabled in Parliament in April, following his marriage to Caroline of Brunswick.*

**Diamond Cut Diamond – Intended as a Frontispiece to the Phamphlet**

15 August 1806

WILLIAMS

*In 1801 a jeweller, Nathanial Jeffrey, published the debts owing to him by the Prince of Wales, which amounted to £16,808. This public shaming had no effect and so in 1806 Jeffrey published a pamphlet setting out all the transactions he had undertaken with the Prince and Mrs Fitzherbert. It explained why Jeffrey had to be made bankrupt in 1799. Quite apart from not paying for the jewelry made for his wedding to Caroline, or for presents to his mother and sisters, George had also borrowed from Jeffrey. The pamphlet excited a riposte, probably encouraged by George, entitled 'Diamond cut Diamond' and so here George is shown about to settle a bill of £400 to an ingratiating Jeffrey. The pamphlet had no effect, for nothing was paid.*

**Leap Year, or, John Bull's Peace Establishment**

March 1816

WILLIAMS

*Prince Leopold, handsome but penniless, met Princess Charlotte, George's daughter, for the first time on 27 February 1816 and on 15 March their marriage settlement was laid before Parliament – £60,000 a year, £10,000 for the Princess, and £60,000 for dresses, jewels and furniture. Poor John Bull has to carry all this on top of the taxes to pay for the controversial navy and army estimates after the war was over. George encourages Charlotte, who is clearly in charge, with the advice he had always followed: 'Push on! Preach Economy! And when you have got your money follow my example—'*

## Economical Humbug of 1816, or, Saving at the Spiggot and Letting Out at the Bunghole

28 April 1816

GEORGE CRUIKSHANK

*John Bull watches in puzzled bewilderment as the Chancellor of the Exchequer, Vansittart, shows him the tiny amount of money that flows from the National Exchequer to public services, while a torrent of gold gushes into the hands of the Regent and his friends. Prince Leopold is holding a tub marked '£60,000 for fun', and John Nash, the architect, has a tub for 'Cottages and Pavilions'.*

John Bull brought up for his Discharge but Remanded on account of Extravagance & False Schedule

**John Bull Brought Up for His Discharge But Remanded on Account of Extravagance and False Schedule**

29 March 1817

ISAAC AND GEORGE CRUIKSHANK

*Following the war there was real agricultural and industrial distress, with poor harvests and unemployment caused by the use of new machinery. Three ministers – Castlereagh, Canning and Eldon – try to show that Government debt was due principally to the expenses of the war and maintaining an army and navy. The figures in the schedule are items relating to those expenses and to the support for Britain's allies. However, the Prince Regent is also in the dock, having to answer to poor and ragged citizens.*

# 3 The Roving Eye

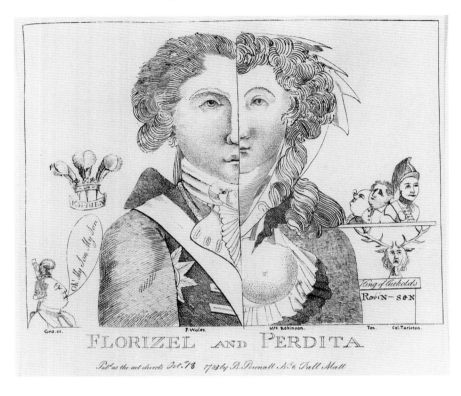

FLORIZEL AND PERDITA

*Pub.<sup>d</sup> as the act directs Oct.<sup>r</sup> 18 1783 by B. Pownall No.6 Pall Mall*

## Florizel and Perdita

18 October 1783

*The seventeen-year-old George had fallen for Mary Robinson, the leading lady at Drury Lane, where she played Perdita in Garrick's adaptation of* The Winter's Tale. *The twenty-three-year-old wife of an Irish actor, she was a celebrity who, like Madonna today, was pursued by the press and became a glamorous idol of the masses. She modestly claimed in her memoirs, 'Whenever I appeared in public I was overwhelmed by the gazing of the multitude.' For George it was a passionate, short-lived, and very expensive affair. This print may be misdated as the affair took place three years earlier, or it may have been published to refresh the public's memory of George the seducer as the political crisis of 1783–84 unfolded. Perdita was still a fashion icon who sported the buff and blue colours of the Whigs.*

BY THE AGE OF SIXTEEN George had become a very handsome boy and he had probably lost his virginity to the tall, pretty wife of one of the grooms who had been promoted to a job within the Household so that she could be close to the Prince. In the summer of 1778 he fell madly in love with Mary Hamilton, the twenty-three-year-old attendant to his sisters, who was a relative of the Duke of Hamilton. He wrote passionate letters to her almost every day, a practice that he followed repeatedly in his various amours – his pen invariably preceded his penis. Mary held him at bay, as she prized her virtue. In December 1779 the King and Queen took George to Drury Lane, where his roving eye turned towards the popular, young and very attractive actress Mary Robinson.

Mary was the mistress of George's twenty-two-year-old friend Lord Malden, who had set her up in a house in Clarges Street and given her a silk-lined carriage in which she drove around the fashionable streets of London. Perhaps she drew too much attention to herself by flirting with other gallants, but in the case of the Prince Malden was quite content to surrender him to her expert charms. She was the star of Drury Lane, and appeared as Perdita in *The Winter's Tale*. George, ever adept with his pen, started to write to her, signing himself Florizel. A daily bombardment of letters offering, amongst other things, a bond of £20,000 when he came of age persuaded her to give up her career as an actress and become his mistress.

The printmakers and balladeers, who were the paparazzi of the day, had great fun in exposing this relationship. One of the broadsides carried these verses:

> Sometimes she'd play the tragic queen,
> Sometimes the peasant poor.
> Sometimes she'd step behind the scene
> And there she'd play the w——.
>
> Two thousand pounds, a princely sight!
> For doing just no more
> Than what is acted every night
> By every sister w——.
>
> She never played her part so well
> In all her life before,
> Yet some, as well as Florizel,
> Know how she plays the w——.

**THE COCK of the WALK, DISTRIBUTING HIS FAVOURS.**

## The Cock of the Walk Distributing his Favours

31 May 1786

G. TOWNLY STUBBS

*In this rare print, George is a cock that has lost all its feathers (a fact noted by a laughing oyster-woman) because he has given them away as favours to his various paramours – the Duchess of Devonshire, Lady Melbourne, Mrs Vanneck, Lady Maitland and, on the floor, Mrs Fitzherbert. Mrs Vanneck was mentioned*

*by Horace Walpole in 1795 as one of the Prince's court at Brighton. Lady M—d could be the wife of Viscount Maitland, one of Fox's martyrs (losers at the 1784 election), 'a nice little painted doll'. George's team are Weltje drawing the barrow and Hanger acting as a middleman picking out the favours labelled 'To the D—ss of D—e'. The three heads – of Burke, Fox and North – are like a pawnbroker's sign above the Fores print shop, which has other prints in the window:* The Royal Toast *[page 84] and* His Highness in Fitz *[page 88].*

Within a few months George's eye had settled on another courtesan, Mrs Grace Dalrymple Elliott, known as 'Dally the Tall', the wife of an impoverished doctor. Lord Malden was summoned to negotiate terms of settlement with Mary Robinson and, in particular, the return of his love letters, which she was threatening to publish. The Prince gave her a pay-off of £5,000 and a pension of £500 a year. As a celebrated lady of the town Mary was painted by Romney, Hoppner and Reynolds. Gainsborough's portrait of her was proudly displayed in Carlton House. Later paralysed from the waist down, she took to writing poems and novels. She remained on quite good terms with George, who led the list of subscribers to her volume of poems in 1791. She became a close friend of Coleridge and when she died in 1800 George paid the annuity, though at a reduced level, to her daughter.

In 1794 George's eye strayed again, from Mrs Fitzherbert, his established partner, to settle on Frances, Countess of Jersey, a very attractive woman of forty-one, a mother to eight children and a grandmother. She was an experienced paramour who slept around with several lords, earls and dukes, but her ambition was now fixed on the heir to the throne. A contemporary believed her to be a serpent: 'beautiful, bright, and glossy in its exterior – in its interior poisonous and pestiferous.' A contemporary piece of doggerel gave George's view:

> I've kissed and I've prattled with fifty granddames
> And changed them as oft, do ye see,
> But of all the grandmammies that dance on the Steine,
> The widow of Jersey give me.

## Fashionable Jockeyship

1 June 1796

JAMES GILLRAY

*George, wearing his adored uniform of Colonel of the Tenth Regiment of Light Dragoons, known as 'The Prince of Wales's Own', rides Lord Jersey, holding his queue of hair as a rein. The Prince had appointed him Master of the Horse, and this willing cuckold leads the Prince to the bed of his wife, Frances, Countess of Jersey. This affair had started in 1794 and now Lady Jersey was at the height of her power, comforting the Prince of Wales a few days after his marriage to Caroline. The picture on the wall of Cupid playing to an old sow with distended udders reminded the public that Lady Jersey was older than George, a mother of eight, and a grandmother.*

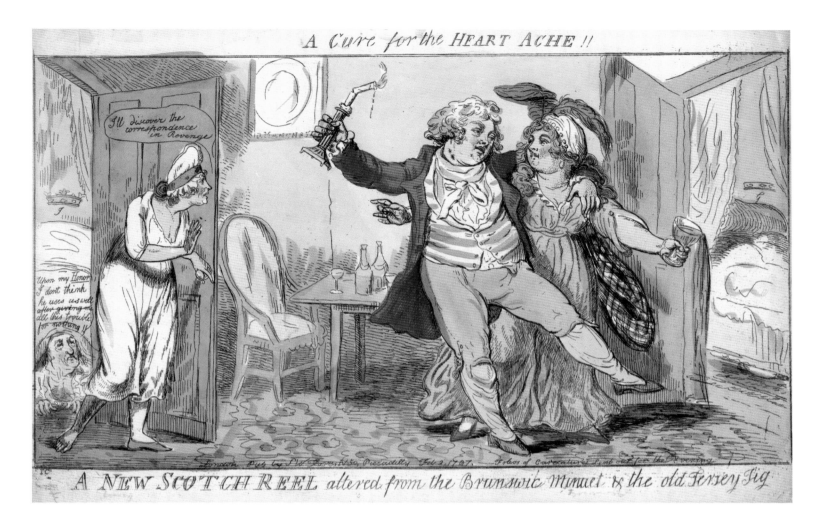

A Cure for the HEART ACHE!!

I'll discover the correspondence in Revenge

Upon my Honor I dont think he uses us well after giving me all this trouble for nothing!!

A NEW SCOTCH REEL altered from the Brunswic Minuet & the old Jersey Jig

George could not restrain his lust and became so besotted with her that he even dismissed John Payne, Comptroller of the Household, and Thomas Tyrwhitt, his Private Secretary, both of whom had dared to criticize her and spoken up for Caroline. Lady Jersey was credited with having persuaded George to find a wife on two accounts – it would be one in the eye for Maria Fitzherbert, and it would serve as a shield for their own adultery. Some years later Wellington went further and alleged that Lady Jersey had chosen Caroline for George in the hope that 'disgust for the wife would secure constancy to the mistress'.

Such was the hold of Lady Jersey over George that with callous insensitivity he appointed her to be one of Caroline's Ladies of the Bedchamber. In that role she constantly undermined Caroline, passed malicious gossip back to George, and ensured that her charms were ever available when he recoiled with disgust from his wife. She became a figure that the public

## A New Scotch Reel Altered from the Brunswick Minuet and the Old Jersey Jig

2 February 1797

ISAAC CRUIKSHANK

*The days of Lady Jersey are over and the tipsy, dishevelled Prince is being lured away from her bedroom – where her husband laments that they have 'got nothing' – to the bedroom of the Duchess of Manchester. George was incapable of maintaining a steady relationship with one woman, for at the same time he was also having affairs with Honor Gullons, who lived in Bath, and Eliza Crole, who gave birth to a son named George in 1799. The boy was almost certainly George's son – he was given help in his military career and on the King's death was sent £10,000 by the Duke of Wellington, one of the King's executors, 'for a natural son of George IV'.*

ALL for LOVE, or the modern David and Goliah

## All for Love, or, The Modern David and Goliah

December 1806

WILLIAMS

*The* Rising Sun, *a scurrilous magazine, carried the story that George, while staying at the house of his friend Michael Angelo Taylor, seduced the man's wife, Frances Ann. Here Taylor horsewhips the Prince, who is fleeing in his nightshirt and depicted as Falstaff. Taylor was very short and very pompous – he sat for seven seats in the House and was active in the Whig interest. His inherited wealth allowed his attractive wife to be a leading Whig hostess at their house, Privy Gardens, Whitehall. Until 1812 he was an intimate of the Prince of Wales, who professed that he 'loved no man so well', but after the Whigs had been overlooked he became more aligned with the Opposition.*

loved to hate – burnt as a scarecrow in Brighton, and forced to flee her house in Pall Mall when it was threatened by a mob. The King insisted in 1796 that she be removed from Caroline's household and in the next year George, tiring of her carnal delights, dropped her. Two years later George sacked her husband as Master of the Horse. When George's ardour cooled he could be very spiteful: he later warned his daughter not to get too close to the 'Jezebel' Lady Jersey.

In 1799 George was reconciled with Maria Fitzherbert and they resumed a regular companionship that lasted for several years. However, in 1806 George's tirelessly roving eye settled upon Isabella, Marchioness of Hertford. She was younger than Maria but two years older than George and, like her predecessor, a mother and even a grandmother of twelve years. A verse pamphlet captured George's predilection for ample dowagers:

> The foremost of the r—— brood
> Who broke his shell and cried for food
> Turned out a cock of manners rare,
> A fav'rite with the feathered fair…

> But though his love was sought by all,
> Game, dunghill, bantam, squab and tall,
> Among the whole, not one in ten,
> Could please him like a tough old hen.

Lady Hertford, unlike Lady Jersey, had a very rich husband who had a passion for French furniture and fine paintings, and many of the pieces he collected can be seen today at the Wallace Collection at their house in Manchester Square. George soon fell completely under her sway and persuaded himself that he couldn't possibly live without her – 'he frets himself into a fever to persuade Lady Hertford to live with him publicly.' When she was not around he was tearful and depressed, moping about Carlton House simply doing nothing. He wrote to her every day and when she was in London he visited her every day.

Many were amazed at the hold she had over George. She was not particularly attractive, 'the most forbidding, haughty and unpleasant-looking woman' according to one contemporary; another found her 'stately, formal, insipid'. It seeems she was not very passionate and it is probable that she did not fully

## The Royal Milling Match

December 1811

*George had sprained his ankle teaching his daughter to dance the Highland Fling. Lampooners quickly connected this accident to the supposed attention that George was paying to Lady Yarmouth, the daughter-in-law of his mistress Lady Hertford. Here Lord Yarmouth punches him on the nose, warning George not to 'poach'. This accusation, like many of the rumours about George and his amours, had no foundation, and this is the only print to allege it.*

> *Frantic with joy, the fair one ey'd*
> *Her faithful Y—H at her side;*
> *And quickly to his ear repeated,*
> *How by the P—E she had been treated.*
>
> *The peer's indignant feelings rose,*
> *And words were soon exchang'd for blows*
> *No rebel eloquence he tries,*
> *But boldly blacks the gallant's eyes.*
>
> *In vain the P—E for mercy cry'd;*
> *'Perfidious man!' the peer reply'd;*
> *'Presum'st thou thus my friend to use,*
> *My honour and my love abused!'*

## Patent Puppets Alias the Hertford Fantoccini

April 1812

WILLIAMS(?)

*This print attacks the supposed influence of Lady Hertford in George's decision to keep Perceval in office. Her right hand holds the four strings controlling the Perceval puppet. The spurned Whig puppets are hung on a peg behind her. A puzzled John Bull says 'what a clever leady thee must be'. Isabella plays her part in this Regency Theatre as 'Performer to His Royal Highness'.*

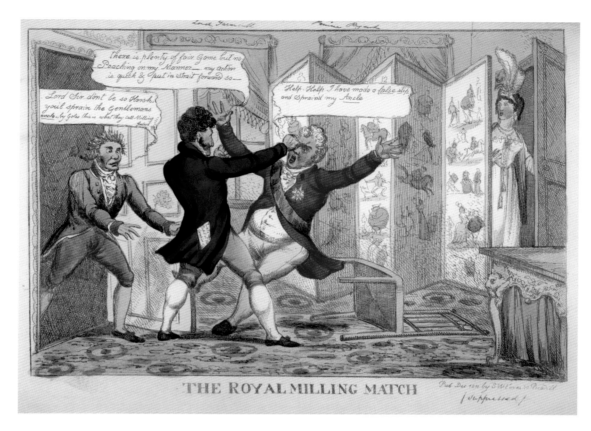

THE ROYAL MILLING MATCH

PATENT PUPPETS alias the HERTFOD FANTOCCINI.

STATE MYSTERIES

**State Mysteries, a Vision of Pall Mall**

1 April 1813

WILLIAMS

*This appeared in the satirical magazine, the* Scourge. *It comments upon the investigation in 1806 that followed the accusations by Sir John and Lady Douglas, formerly Caroline's friends at Blackheath, of her alleged debauchery. Here Caroline is led by Truth, who is shining a mirror into George's face. Envy flinches and tries to hide her head. The Douglases are alarmed but it is Lady Hertford's position that is astonishing: she is taking refuge by hiding her head in the Regent's groin – an implication that he enjoyed fellation.*

VISION of PALL MALL.

Pub.ᵈ April 1ˢᵗ 1813 by W.N. Jones Newgate Street

become his mistress. Above all George wanted a sympathetic companion, a ready listener to whom he could pour out his heart. Lady Hertford's children and her husband frequently joined them for dinner. George yearned for the ease and comfort of family life, and this is what the Hertfords provided.

Isabella Hertford had a considerable influence on George's political decisions. She reinforced his growing conservatism and she is credited in the prints with George's decision to retain Perceval and the Tories in office when he became Regent. Her influence extended until 1820.

In 1819 George spied another fat matron of fifty, Elizabeth, Lady Conyngham. She had led a colourful life – one of her previous lovers had also shared Lady Jersey's bed and she was rumoured to have seduced the future Tsar Nicholas I on his visit to England in 1816. Within a few months she had insinuated herself into the Prince's life, choosing his Pages for the

## He Stoops to Conquer, or, Royal George Sunk!

March 1819

LEWIS MARKS

*One night in March George, who was immensely proud of the kitchens in the Brighton Pavilion, decided to dine there and the red carpet was rolled out. When the* Brighton Herald *reported this the printmakers had a field day. George is turning his phallic attention to a fat cook-maid who hopes, while protecting her honour with a soup cover, that by pandering to the royal spit she might become a countess. In the background Bloomfield, his Private Secretary, and Yarmouth are also busy seducing the staff.*

## Royal Hobby's, or, The Hertfordshire Cock-horse

20 April 1819

GEORGE CRUIKSHANK

*In this striking image George rides one of the new velocipedes, carrying as his passenger Isabella Hertford. Even he is complaining about her weight. In the background the Duke of York rejoices that on their mother's death George had given him a sinecure worth £10,000 a year, a naked bit of jobbery which had been attacked in the Commons.*

## K—G Cupid in the Corner – Playing Bopeep

16 September 1820

WILLIAM ELMES

*Within a matter of months, Lady Conyngham had completely captivated George. She provided comfort and protection during the divorce proceedings with Caroline. Here he hides under Lady Conyngham's skirt – a position he describes as paradise. George became so dependent upon her that she was often referred to as Vice-Queen, or Mrs Queen. She is saying 'Heigh Ho for petticoat government.' In the picture hanging on the wall all the men, including the King, are cuckolded.*

coronation, and throwing kisses to the new King during the ceremony. Like Lord Jersey and Lord Hertford before him, Lord Conyngham asked for and was given an official position: he sought not only to advance himself but to become as rich as he could by condoning the adultery of his wife.

The customary pattern soon followed. George could not bear to be without Lady Conyngham and she systematically exploited her position by getting jobs for her family and former lovers. She was vain and rapacious, with a great love for jewelry. Between 1821 and 1829 George spent over £100,000 at the royal jewellers, principally on gifts for her – she particularly liked pearls and was given a necklace valued at £3,150. Princess de Lieven, wife of the Russian ambassador in London, remarked, 'Not an idea in her head, not a word to say for herself; nothing but a hand to accept pearls and diamonds with, and an enormous balcony to wear them on.'

At this latter stage of his life George needed the comfort of a nurse and companion, and he was quite happy to rest cradled on the ample bosom of Lady Conyngham. When he died she loaded up a carriage with as much booty as she could from Windsor and drove off with it – but she was forced to return the Stuart Sapphire, a large gem previously owned by Princess Charlotte that is now set at the back of the British Imperial State Crown.

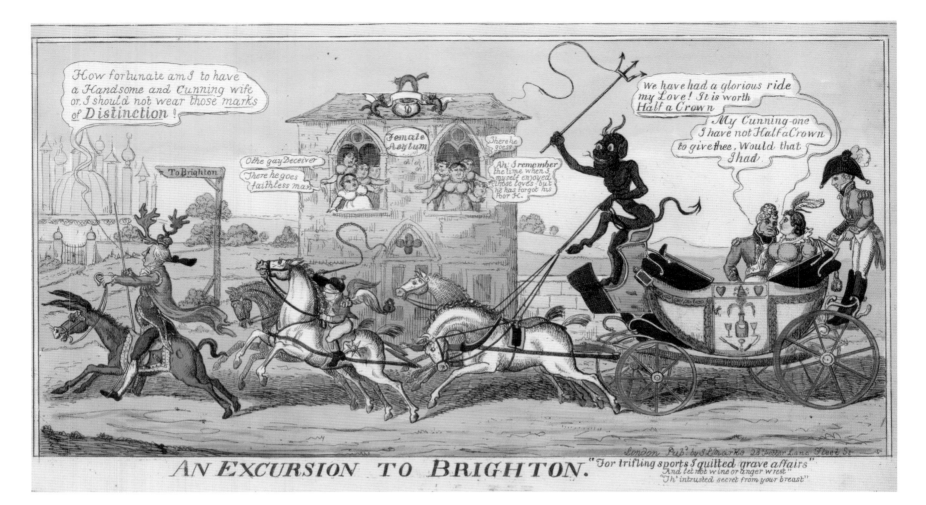

AN EXCURSION TO BRIGHTON.

## An Excursion to Brighton

September 1820

LEWIS MARKS

*In a barouche driven by the Devil, George carries off his new mistress, the fat Lady Conyngham, to Brighton, with Cupid riding postillion and her husband riding an ass. George's former mistresses barrack him from a 'Female Asylum'. During his divorce trial it had slowly become known that George had moved on from Isabella Hertford, but not amongst the mob, which shattered the windows of her house rather than those of Lady Conyngham's. This scene is directly borrowed from a George Cruikshank caricature that appeared in the* Scourge *of October 1812,* An Excursion to Ragley Hall, *in which Lord Hertford leads a procession taking his wife and George to his country estate.*

## Sultan Sham and his Seven Wives

1820

LEWIS MARKS

*George struts past his harem of not very recognizable paramours saying 'Variety is charming. Constance is not for me, so Ladies pray take warning.' This was the frontispiece to a poem supporting Caroline and listing all George's affairs in considerable and remarkably accurate detail:*

> *Now the Vice Sultan look'd around,*
> *And in a little time he found*
> *Another wife, a fifth, they say,*
> *Mature in years, tho' brisk and gay:*
> *She had a husband, was a granny,*
> *Tho' still libidinous as any…*

**The Blanket Hornpipe**

September 1820

WILLIAM ELMES

*Some of George's paramours revenge themselves by tossing him in a blanket. A bubbling Caroline says, 'We will not spare him'; Lady Jersey, 'Oh base be his name'; and Lady Hertford, 'We will give him Pains and Penalties.' Two soldiers cheer on the ladies. The Blanket Hornpipe was a farce playing in London.*

A WINDSOR PA(EA)IR, FULL RIPE

## A Windsor Pa(ea)ir, Full Ripe

1 April 1828

THOMAS JONES

*The last woman to comfort George was a beautiful young actress, Eliza Chester, who was given the job of Reader to the King with a salary of £600. George had abandoned Brighton and Carlton House and was now living at the Royal Lodge in the middle of Windsor Great Park, originally designed as a thatched cottage orné by Nash but extensively and extravagantly developed by Wyatville. It was George's last great theatrical adventure in architecture.*

## King Henry IV

June 1827

WILLIAM HEATH

*Both George and Lady Conyngham were immensely fat. Here George, as Falstaff, is saying to her, as Doll Tearsheet, 'I am old, I am old.' She replies, 'I love thee better than I love e'er a scurvy young boy of them all.' An eyewitness, Mrs Charles Arbuthnot, recorded, 'They spend the evening sitting on a sofa together holding each other's hands, whispering and kissing,*

KING HENRY IV.

*Lord C. being present.' He is indeed present here below the cuckold's horns as Mistress Quickly. Greville, the Clerk to the Privy Council, records a comment heard at White's that 'She has a leg like a post' to which Copley, later Lord Chancellor, replied, 'A poste Royale.'*

# 4 The Darling of the Opposition

BY 1780 CHARLES JAMES FOX had established himself as the most compelling, most witty orator in the House of Commons, building his reputation on a series of impromptu and scathing speeches on Lord North's conduct of the American war. He gathered around him a group of Whigs who were not only disappointed at being denied any office for over twenty years, but who were also supporters of radical ideas and resented the powers of the Crown. Fox's father had amassed a vast fortune through jobbery, but his son, a gregarious, womanizing gamester, had run through it very quickly, and by 1781 his main income came from a twelfth share in the profits of the faro bank at Brooks's, plus six guineas an hour when he dealt. He established his base at the club in St James's, which, always more than a gaming club, became a rendezvous for his followers whenever there was a crisis.

The Prince of Wales was drawn to Fox, not only because of his coolness towards the King – he happily joined in a toast to 'The Majesty of the People' – but because of his expansive, wayward charm. Fox was well educated, being a Classical scholar, and he was able to talk about Italian artists with knowledge and a feeling just as discriminating as the Prince's. Gambling and beautiful women were also common interests. Fox took on Perdita as one of his mistresses after she had been cast off by the Prince of Wales, and he soon established a permanent relationship with Mrs Elizabeth Armistead, a tall, beautiful cockney who had herself succumbed to the lust of the young Prince. Fox was to marry her in 1795, but he kept the marriage secret until 1802. The Prince had shared with Fox his women, his wine and his gambling, but there was much more to their relationship: it was a common political purpose that brought them together.

In the 18th century politicians out of office were attracted to the heirs to the throne because they offered the prospect of office in the future with a change in regime. By 1782 the Prince had established in Carlton House, at the other end of the Mall from Buckingham House, an alternative Court to which Fox was ever-welcome. It was an open secret, as Horace Walpole recorded in March 1783, that 'The Prince of Wales has had [sic] of late thrown himself into the arms of Charles James Fox.'

## Falstaff and his Prince

16 May 1783

JOHN BOYNE

*This is the first print to compare the relationship of George and Charles James Fox to that of Falstaff and Prince Hal. Fox asks the Prince for money, offering George his hand and his mistress Mrs Armistead. The comparison was apt: Fox and Falstaff were men of great girth, with warm hearts and beguiling charm. Through all the political vicissitudes of the next twenty-three years George retained affection for the companion of his youth, and when he heard of Fox's death he broke down and wept. Shakespeare does not describe Henry V's reaction to Falstaff's death, but Nym's comment, 'The King hath run bad humours on the Knight', indicates that it was not as spontaneous and warm as George's. In reply to Maria Fitzherbert, who had reminded him how Prince Hal had abandoned Falstaff, George wrote that he liked Shakespeare, particularly Henry IV, which he knew well.*

## The Countryman's Dream of Coalescing Virtue and Vice

20 March 1784

WILLIAM DENT

*Many thought that the Young Pitt would not survive as Prime Minister and expected it was only a matter of time before North and Fox would return to power. The country gentlemen even hoped for a Pitt–Fox coalition. Here North holds the infant Pitt as Fox, Thurlow, Burke, Shelburne, Richmond and Portland dance around the regal maypole. The Prince of Wales beats his drum, delighted at the prospect of Fox coming back. But Pitt survived several votes in the Commons in February and March: on 24 March he was able to secure dissolution of Parliament – now the electors were to decide.*

## The Introduction of F—— to St James's

3 May 1786

*This takes the implications of George's secret marriage much further into the political arena. Maria Fitzherbert is in charge, borne on George's shoulders, for she has become the inspiration and mascot of the Opposition. In the procession down Pall Mall to St James's Palace, Hanger leads with a drum, North plays the horn, Fox the cornet, and Burke, in his Jesuit biretta, the fife. For the Whigs Maria was a mixed blessing: a rallying point to support George, but also a political embarrassment, for George had spurned Fox's pleas not to marry her.*

THE COUNTRYMAN'S DREAM OF COALESCING VIRTUE AND VICE.

*Round about the Maypole see how we trot, hot pot, hot, brown Ale we have got — — — — — — — Midas.*

THE INTRODUCTION OF F—— TO St. JAMES'S.

HONOR. AND. HONESTY.

LOVE. AND. LOYALTY.

FITZ AND GOOD COMPANY.

## THE GENERAL TOAST.

Published by S. W. Fores October 20 1786, at the caricature warehouse nᵒ 3 Piccadilly.

### The General Toast

20 October 1786

*This rare print features three ironic toasts: Fox with dice and the Knave of Clubs (sometimes he was depicted as the Knave of Hearts) is toasted with 'Honor and Honesty'; the reformer John Wilkes squints as he pens another attack on George III, 'Love and Loyalty'; and George and Maria, gazing fondly at each other with her hand around his neck, are toasted with 'Fitz and Good Company'. Their book is the bawdy songs of George's crony Charles Morris.*

The direct issue that brought them together was the financial settlement for the Prince on his coming of age. The Prime Minister, the Duke of Portland, was quite willing to grant an annual sum of £100,000 but George III thought it to be 'a shameful squandering of money'. Fox, now a Secretary of State, was happy to take up the Prince's cause, though to no effect.

Fox was about to fall from power as he had introduced a Bill to reform the Government of India but its real target was the misuse of the wealth and patronage of the East India Company. The King let it be known that anyone who supported the Bill was not his friend, and it was defeated in the House of Lords by nineteen votes. The King dismissed Fox, North and Portland on 18 December 1783 and appointed as First Lord of the Treasury the twenty-four-year-old second son of the Earl of Chatham – William Pitt, who had led the opposition to Fox's India Bill.

After precariously surviving a number of parliamentary votes Pitt decided to call a general election in the spring of 1784. The contest in Westminster was the most caricatured of any in the 18th century. The King ordered the members of his Household and the Brigade of Guards to vote for the Tory; the twenty-six-year-old Duchess of Devonshire canvassed the publicans, butchers and tradesmen of Westminster offering kisses for a vote for Fox. Fox's followers flaunted the colours of buff and blue – the colours of Washington's volunteers. When Fox's victory was declared there was a great parade, which was joined by the Prince's carriage and twenty-four gentlemen of his Household, and the Prince sported Fox's favours in his hat (a laurel wreath and a fox's brush). Nine marquees were put up on the great lawns of Carlton House and George hosted a dinner in Fox's honour. Later they went on to a ball given by the celebrated hostess Mrs Crewe, the wife of a Foxite MP. The Prince gave the toast 'Here's buff and blue and Mrs Crewe,' to which Mrs Crewe replied, 'Here's buff and blue and all of you.' But Fox's victory in Westminster was the only star in the Whig firmament: many Whigs lost their seats (Fox's martyrs) and Pitt won an overall majority in the House of Commons. For many years after, George found Fox and Sheridan not only congenial companions but useful allies in his long, sapping relationship with his father; but the peak of their influence was the Regency Crisis of 1788–89.

In 1792 George, in his maiden speech in the House of Lords defending Pitt's Bill to restrict seditious writings, praised England's 'great and sacred constitution', which he declared he would defend to his dying day. The execution of Louis XVI and the declaration of war in 1793 easily persuaded George to believe that everything that France stood for had to be annihilated – while Fox continued to believe that the revolutionaries were right to purge France of the Bourbons. George was much more in tune with the feeling of the country and the coolness and distancing from Fox and Sheridan continued through most of the 1790s, only ending when they were invited to dine with him in 1797. By that time, as George failed to receive a high military appointment he had hoped for from his father, it was time again to find some allies in the ranks of the Opposition.

A few days after Pitt told the King in 1801 that he was going to resign, George III succumbed to another attack of porphyria. It was relatively mild but lasted for several weeks, during which the Prince of Wales set about forming his government-in-waiting – Fox was to be Home Secretary; Grey the Secretary of State for War; and, as a real turn-up for financial orthodoxy, Sheridan was to become Chancellor of the Exchequer. The Whigs' expectations of rewards at last were dashed as the King recovered sufficiently to appoint Addington, another Tory, First Lord of the Treasury.

Again, in 1804, the King fell ill. This time it was more serious as he needed to be put into a straitjacket and was unable to perform any royal duties for five months. At times not even the Queen was allowed to see him and the Prince of Wales complained that by being specifically excluded from seeing his father he was not able to discover how ill he really was. Thomas Creevey recorded in his diary that 'During the Autumn of 1805 the Prince considered himself as the head of the Whig Party' and George set about forming a new government, seeking the advice of Thurlow, the Lord Chancellor whom Pitt had sacked. This only confirmed Pitt's belief that the Prince was 'the worst anchoring ground in Europe'.

Addington found it difficult to command a majority in the House and the King recognized that there was no alternative but to recall Pitt – a move much welcomed by Caroline, the Princess of Wales, who said she was 'proud to name herself a Pittite'. Pitt again galvanized the nation to resist Napoleon, but his lifelong addiction to claret and port led to his early death through cirrhosis of the liver in 1806.

Here was an opportunity for the Prince of Wales. The King called upon the Grenville family, who had been regular guests to dinners at Carlton House, to form an administration that came to be known as 'The Ministry of All the Talents' as well as – due to their huge girth – 'The Broad Bottom Ministry'. Several Whigs were included – Grey was First Lord of the Admiralty;

Falstaff & The Merry Wives of WESTMINSTER, Canvasing for Their FAVORITE MEMBER L.ᴰ T—ᴰ

### Falstaff and the Merry Wives of Westminster Canvassing for their Favourite Member Ld T—d

20 July 1788

JOHN BOYNE

*Hood's appointment as Lord of the Admiralty caused a by-election in Westminster – Fox's land. His candidate was Lord Townshend, who was also an amateur caricaturist. Here he is supported by the bare-breasted Lady Portland and Lady Rutland – whom Townshend had allegedly seduced, hence the name 'Rut' on her belt. This print reawakens the comparison of Fox and George to Falstaff and Prince Hal. Here the Prince of Wales is the ass being ridden by Fox. Huge sums were spent on the by-election, sailors rioted in Covent Garden, and Townshend won by a narrow margin: a bad result for Pitt.*

## The Grand Review on Sydenham Common

28 June 1792

ISAAC CRUIKSHANK

*With war with France in the offing, George III reviewed the troops on Sydenham Common. The Prince of Wales attended; here he is being put to flight with his companions Fox, Grey and Sheridan. This is unfair because on 21 May the Prince, in the House of Lords, had supported Pitt's proclamation proposing measures against British radicals and thus had distanced himself from the Whigs. It took some time for this to be recognized by a wider public. The Duke of York was in charge of the troops on the day and this emphasizes again that George, the Prince of Wales, had been denied any significant military role by his father.*

The GRAND REVIEW on SYDENHAM COMMON

*The Prince and his party were drove to the Summit of a hill where they made a stand for nearly an hour & a half but where at length Obliged to retreat to the bottom setting fire to the furze & hedges the Smoke of wh favoured their flight & left the several battalions masters of the field his Majesty followed the enemy on foot at the head of a troop of dragoons to the foot of the hill when he remounted & returned back to the lines*

FALSE LIBERTY REJECTED or Fraternizing & Equalizing PRINCIPLES DISCARDED

In the Exhibition is a Complete Model of the Guillotine. No more COALITIONS no more FRENCH CUT THROATS.

Fox was Foreign Secretary; and Sheridan got a minor post in the Admiralty. The only close crony of George to be in the Cabinet was Lord Moira, who was fobbed off with the post of Master General of the Ordnance. George pressed hard for honours, posts and baronetcies for his friends but he got little and he was angry that Grenville decided to do nothing about his debts.

'The Broad Bottom Ministry' never recovered from the death of Fox in September 1806. It, too, fell out with the King over the Catholic question, which led to the return of a Tory administration under Portland, and later under Perceval.

The death of Fox deprived the Whigs of their most charismatic figure and also George of one of his oldest and closest friends in the world of politics. For over twenty-five years they had shared many interests and they had heard the chimes at

## False Liberty Rejected, or, Fraternizing and Equalizing Principles Discarded

7 March 1793

ISAAC CRUIKSHANK

*By supporting the proclamation against seditious writings in his maiden speech to the House of Lords, George had effectively turned his back on Fox, Sheridan and the Whigs. His aim was to win over George III to allow him to serve abroad and to help him once again with his debts. The King welcomes the prodigal, who uses the words of Prince Hal in* Henry IV *when he dismisses 'the Tutors and the Feeders of my Riots'. It was not until 1797 – some four years later – that Fox was invited to dine at Carlton House.*

Achitophel, an old Jew Scribe lately turn'd Greek.     Greeks.     Persians (stowed together) worshipping the rising Sun

## Achitophel, an Old Jew Scribe Lately Turned Greek; Greeks; Persians (Stowed Together) Worshipping the Rising Sun

11 July 1804

JAMES SAYERS

*With the prospect of a Regency, Thurlow, the Chancellor whom Pitt had sacked, is depicted as Achitophel, the biblical conspirator who turned against David. He looks on expectantly while Fox and Sheridan instruct the Grenville faction on how to abase themselves before the rising sun (crowned with the Prince of Wales feathers), with Sheridan saying, 'Lower my Lord.' The Grenvilles, whom George had included in his Cabinet dinners at Carlton House, are recognized in cartoons by their large bottoms. The spectacled character is the Duke of Buckingham, who was always lobbying for a government post.*

midnight. Politics for George was always a means of fulfilling his personal ambitions – to pay off his debts; to hold high military rank; to give honours and rewards to his followers; and to ever ready himself to take over from his ill and ageing father. He expected his friends to further these causes.

On Fox's death George wrote to Lord Holland, Fox's nephew, 'the only wish I now feel remaining is that of retiring entirely from all my political career, for in losing Fox we lose everything.' Forbidden by the King from attending Fox's

funeral, he sent instead £500 to help with the cost, and his Volunteer Regiment to help to control the crowds. A few months later he announced that he would be politically neutral: a statement that led many Whigs to charge him with desertion.

The Prince's abandonment of the Whigs was neither sudden nor unexpected. As George grew older he became more conservative and on several occasions in the previous ten years he had found himself out of sympathy with their Francophilia and republican leanings. He had not left them – they had left him.

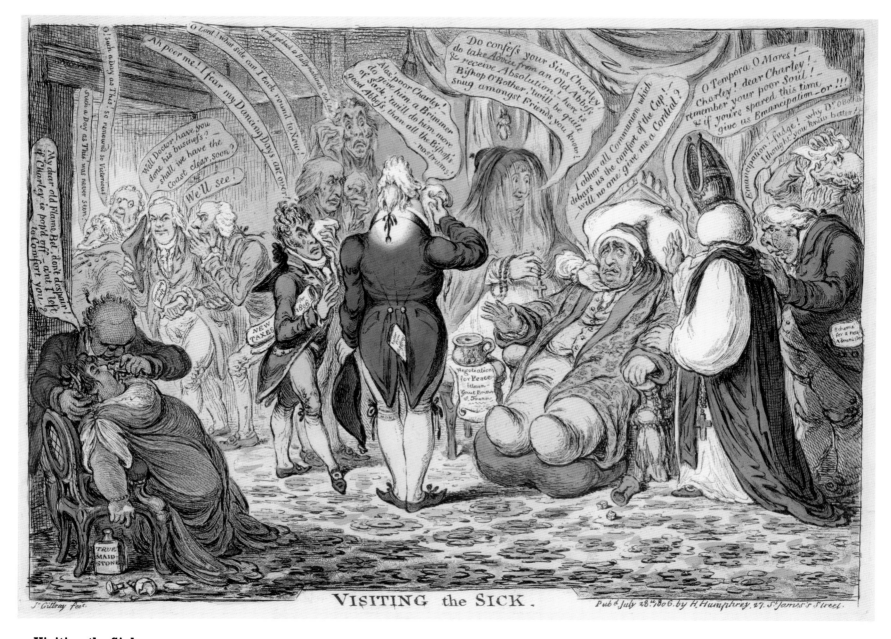

VISITING the SICK.

J. Gillray feet.

Pubd July 28th 1806. by H. Humphrey, 27. St James's Street.

## Visiting the Sick

28 July 1806

JAMES GILLRAY

*Fox fell ill with dropsy in July 1806 and being virtually immobile he was unable to travel to his country house at Chertsey. He had to rest at Chiswick House, which had been lent to him by the Duke of Devonshire, and it was here that he died in September. The Prince could not bring himself to visit Fox as he lay dying so this print shows a fictitious episode.*

*It does, however, accurately reflect the problems facing the crumbling coalition: the Grenvilles are leaving the room with Sidmouth; the Chancellor of the Exchequer, Petty, is considering new taxes; and the issue of Catholic emancipation so dear to Fox, who is egged on by Maria Fitzherbert, is about to destroy the Government. Gillray was astute in ascribing to George the advice to ignore the Catholic bishop and Maria, for this was the issue distancing him from the Whigs. This is the last print by Gillray to include his old target Fox.*

## Carlton House, The Red Drawing Room

1819

W. H. PYNE

*In 1783, Henry Holland, the son of a bricklayer, was commissioned to rebuild Carlton House in the French neoclassical style. For the next nineteen years he was the principal architect of what was to become the most celebrated building in the country.*

*There was a series of sumptuous rooms: the Chinese Room; the Rose Satin Drawing Room; the Velvet Room; the Music Room; two throne rooms; and the Red Drawing Room. Each of these went through many changes – both the upholstery and the silk wall-hangings – from yellow to green and to crimson. In 1809 a Gothic conservatory and a Gothic dining room were added. The distinguished historian of 18th-century architecture, Sir John Summerson, decided that of all George's building projects there were none 'anything as good as Henry Holland's work in Carlton House'. Paintings, clocks, looking glasses, Sèvres china, tapestries, candelabra, chairs, tables and chests were commissioned to adorn this palace.*

*Carlton House was the scene of many parties and the most spectacular fête was held in 1811 to celebrate George's Regency. Over one thousand guests were given dinner, two hundred alone at the Regent's table. Shelley attacked its absurd extravagance: 'It is said that this entertainment will cost £120,000. Nor will it be the last bauble which the nation must buy to amuse this over-grown bantling regency.' George also opened Carlton House for three days and thousands streamed through, gawping in amazement at the furniture and decoration. On the last day a crowd of 30,000 got out of control and several ladies lost their dresses, shoes and hatpins.*

64

# 5 The Would-Be King

IN OCTOBER 1788 George III summoned his physician, Baker, to deal with symptoms of an attack very similar to those he had experienced in 1765 and in 1787. He had acute, crippling stomach and leg pains, and bright red rashes on his arms. Within days this had developed into a fever. He became extremely emotionally disturbed: he interrupted a sermon and shouted at people. The Queen told one of her ladies-in-waiting that his eyes were like blackcurrant jelly, the veins in his face were swollen, the sound of his voice was dreadful: he often spoke until he was exhausted and foam ran out of his mouth. He talked endlessly – one day for nineteen hours – he gave orders to people who did not exist, and offered honours to all and sundry. He was out of his mind.

Of all the various physicians, including one who had advised the Prime Minister, Pitt, not one had any idea what to do. Later medical expertise has diagnosed the illness as a hereditary disorder, porphyria, which can be traced back in the royal family to Mary, Queen of Scots. It was transmitted to the Hanoverians by the Electress Sophia, who was a granddaughter of Mary and the mother of George I. Today the illness is understood and it can be successfully treated, but the only treatments available to George III were bleeding, cupping and purging. Modern research seems to explain why George suffered so terribly from this genetic disorder: his attacks could have been brought on by the presence of arsenic in handcreams, wig powders and 'Grays powders', which were the aspirin of the day.

The Prince of Wales went to Windsor to see his father who, in an outburst of lunatic rage, seized the Prince, hauled him out of his chair, and threw him against a wall. The London newspapers were told it was an attack of gout, and nothing very serious. But the extraordinary nature of the King's illness was slowly getting out. Some believed the King's position was irrecoverable and that he was going to die. Pitt was summoned to a meeting at Windsor in November of 1788 to try to find out the real position.

The following month the King was removed, against his wishes, to Kew. He had become almost unmanageable. Another doctor, Francis Willis, an elderly clergyman who had a reputation for dealing successfully with lunatics, came to see the King. He was the eighth physician to treat the King's case. He had a simple and brutal technique: he put the King in a straitjacket and strapped him into a chair, which came to be known as the Coronation Chair, until the King's fits passed.

Fanny Burney, the Queen's Assistant Keeper of the Robes, recorded where power really lay: 'As the poor King grew worse, a general hope seemed universally to abate and the Prince of Wales took the government of the house [at Windsor] into his own hands.' The Prince's doctor, Richard Warren, believed that the King's disorder would be permanent. It was this great uncertainty that inflamed speculation and encouraged the dawning realization that power might have to pass from father to son. By moving the King to Kew, Pitt had gained the early initiative, but the King's continuing madness caused a major political crisis to develop. Pitt had come to accept by mid-November that there would have to be a regency, with the Prince of Wales as Regent. That would almost certainly end Pitt's tenure as First Lord of the Treasury, for George would appoint his Whig friends. By the end of November it was assumed that Pitt's Government would fall and both *The Times* and *Morning Post* carried the list of the proposed new ministers, headed by Portland as Prime Minister, Fox as Foreign Secretary, Sheridan as Treasurer of the Navy, and Burke as Paymaster of the Forces.

The Prince, at Carlton House, acted as if he were about to become King which, in the circumstances, was not unreasonable. An ugly media war started in London. The Whigs bribed journalists and newspaper publishers to win their support against Pitt, and Whig pamphleteers printed various diagnoses of George III's ailments that indicated it was only a matter of time, possibly a few days, before his son took over. The prints focused on the impetuous eagerness of the Prince to assume royal power. Pitt was supported by the *St James's Chronicle* and the *Crisis*. As *The Times* was on the Government's payroll it attacked George's friends, in particular Weltje, his major-domo in an outburst of racial prejudice calling him 'an itinerant German music-grinder; a great German toad-eater'.

At the start of the crisis Fox had been in Italy, and by the time he returned from Bologna he was suffering from dysentery. He had to leave his sick-bed in order to take part in the famous debate of 10 December 1788. During that debate Fox announced a new constitutional doctrine, that the Prince had

## Dead. Positively Dead

16 November 1788

HENRY KINGSBURY

*This is the first print to expose the crisis created by George III's illness. The Prince tramples on a paper, 'Prayer for the Restorat[io]n his Maj[estys] Health', while Sheridan runs off to find Charles James Fox. Maria Fitzherbert's friends crown her Queen. The Tory Thurlow played a double game – here aligning himself with the Prince's cause by turning his coat – 'This side will do as well as the other.'*

DEAD. POSITIVELY DEAD.

'a right to assume the reins of government and exercise the power of sovereignty'. In effect, the King was dead. This was an astonishing assertion of the hereditary rights of the monarchy and excluded any parliamentary process to regulate the transfer of power or to determine the limitations of that power. Pitt could scarcely conceal his glee that the Whig leader had over-played his hand. Fox, however, had to leave for Bath immediately, to recover his health, and it was left to Sheridan to manoeuvre and plot in London.

London was full of rumours: Mrs Fitzherbert was to become a duchess; the Duke of York to be the Commander-in-Chief; richer pickings and peerages were promised to key supporters; and Whig ladies sported Regency caps decorated with the feathers and motto of the Prince of Wales's badge. In the House of Commons the steadiness of Pitt prevailed and the Opposition was defeated by sixty-four. The importance of this victory was that Pitt had inserted into the Regency Bill a limitation on the power of the Regent to appoint new peers, to award positions and pensions, and that the King's person was to be looked after by the Queen and not the Prince. If there were to be a

regency then it would be a restricted regency. On 12 February 1789 the Regency Bill passed from the Commons to the Lords.

The King's health had been steadily improving and it was possible for his doctors to issue a bulletin that spoke of 'a progressive state of amendment'. Within a week he 'might be said to be well'. The Lord Chancellor told the House of Lords that it was no longer necessary to proceed with the Bill. For a time the Prince of Wales was not allowed to see his father, but eventually a visit was arranged by the Queen, on 23 February, and George, although rather lachrymose himself, saw that the King had recovered his sanity.

The Queen would not easily forgive the conduct of George and his brother, the Duke of York, during her husband's illness, and she virtually ostracized them from Court. She certainly influenced the attitude of George III towards them and the King came to believe they were now part of the Opposition. The mobs in London favoured Pitt and the King, and showed their disapproval of the Prince. On one occasion, when the Prince's carriage was stopped, they tried to get him to shout 'God Bless Pitt.' This was too much for George, who shouted in reply, 'Fox

THE RETURN TO OFFICE.

## The Return to Office

1 July 1811

GEORGE CRUIKSHANK

*In 1809 the Duke of York had been forced to resign as Commander-in-Chief following a scandal involving the sale of military posts, honours, and even a bishopric by his mistress Mrs Clarke, and the Duke's share in the proceeds. The King and Queen had urged George to support his brother, but he hadn't, so to compensate for letting down his family his first act as Regent was to reappoint his brother. Perceval, who had strongly defended the Duke, sweeps away Frederick's accusers, thereby creating another good reason for George to keep him as Prime Minister. As the Duke enters Horse Guards, Fame blows two trumpets, one from his backside.*

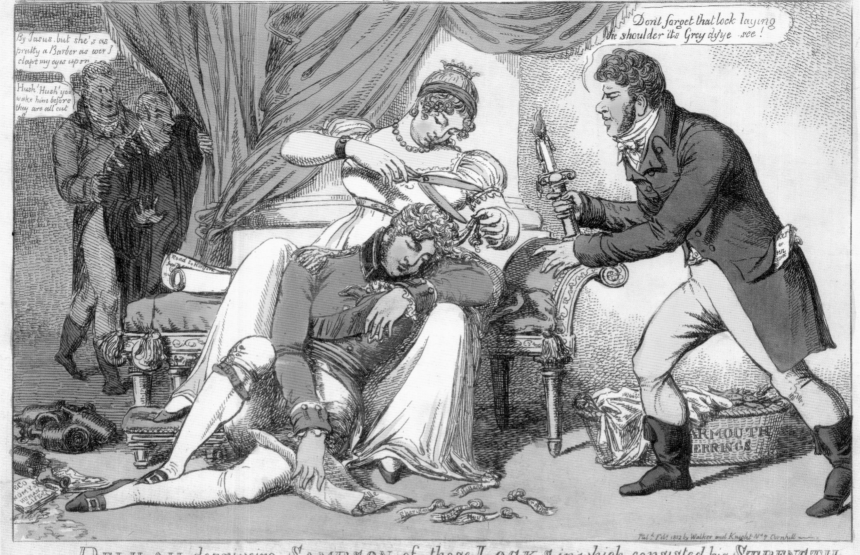

DELILAH *deprweing* SAMPSON *of those* LOCKS *in which consisted his* STRENGTH.

## Delilah Depriving Sampson of those Locks in which Consisted his Strength

February 1812

WILLIAMS

*This is Lady Hertford's first appearance in a print, for it took the caricaturists some years to feature her. She is cutting away the Whig locks from the sleeping Regent. After Fox's death, George distanced himself even more from the Whigs, finding greater sympathy with the attitudes of the Conservatives. In particular, he had a strong personal antipathy to the Whig leader, Grey. In this print Perceval, the Tory Prime Minister, crouches behind the arras and is delighted with Lady Hertford's haircutting.*

*Lord Grey referred in the House of Lords to Isabella Hertford as an 'unseen and separate influence which worked behind the throne – an influence of an odious character, leading to consequences the most pestilent and disgusting.'*

**The Regent's Hack**

March 1812

WILLIAMS

In February, the Prince had decided to retain Perceval in office, and Sheridan, here the hack, was the only Whig to remain faithful to George. Sheridan tells him that he will find a way through the 'ugly road' by kicking away the stones that carry the features of the rejected and disappointed Whigs. At a St Patrick's Day dinner the Prince's name was hissed and Sheridan's defence of him was greeted by angry shouts.

## Polly and Lucy Taking Off the Restrictions

March 1812

GEORGE CRUIKSHANK

*The restrictions on the Regency lapsed in February and here Maria Fitzherbert and Isabella Hertford remove the shackles. In the background Perceval gladly accepts that Grey will not join his administration. The two pictures on the wall of Hanger and Sheridan imply that only George's disreputable friends stayed true to him. The literate buyer of this print would have* *appreciated the allusion to* The Beggar's Opera (1728) by John Gay. *The Regent is Macheath the highwayman, married to the warden's daughter Polly, who was madly in love wiht him – Mrs Fitzherbert. Confined to Newgate, Macheath falls in love with Lucy – Lady Hertford. They vie for his affection. 'How happy could I be with either, Were t'other clear charmed away.' Lucy provided his escape.*

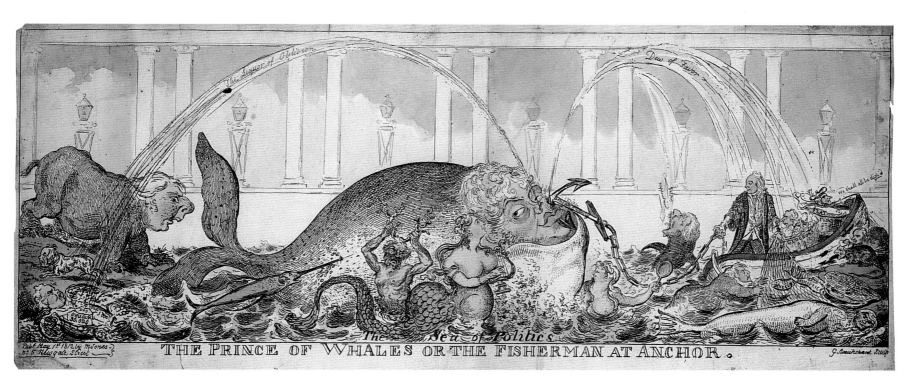

The caption within the image reads: *THE PRINCE OF WHALES OR THE FISHERMAN AT ANCHOR*

**The Prince of Whales, or, The Fisherman at Anchor**

1 May 1812

GEORGE CRUIKSHANK

*This brilliant image was inspired by Charles Lamb's verses in the Examiner of 15 March 1812:*

> *Not a fatter fish than he*
> *Flounders round the polar sea…*
> *Mermaids, with their tails and singing,*
> *His delighted fancy stinging…*
> *For his solace and relief,*
> *Flat-fish are his courtiers chief.*

*It celebrates George's rejection of the Whigs: a great spurt of water lands on Sheridan, a great clumsy animal, and a shower described as a 'Dew of Favour' falls upon Perceval and his ministers. The voluptuous Isabella Hertford catches George's eye while he avoids the mirror of Maria Fitzherbert. The chain by which Perceval has hooked the Prince suggests that Perceval had a blackmailing hold on the Prince – as a result of the Princess of Wales's relationship with Canning, whom Perceval had excluded from his government. (There was a supposition that Canning had been one of Caroline's lovers.)*

# 7 The Happy Husband

**The Royal Toast. Fat, Fair and Forty**

20 March 1786

*This is the first separate print of Mrs Fitzherbert. She was
ample rather than fat, auburn rather than fair, and twenty-nine
not forty, but this phrase stuck.*

IN 1784, AT THE AGE OF TWENTY-THREE, George fell madly in
love with Maria Fitzherbert. She was a beautiful Catholic who
at only twenty-nine had already been twice widowed. Her first
husband, a middle-aged landowner called Edward Weld, died
after falling from a horse in the first year of their marriage. Her
second husband, Thomas Fitzherbert, had died in France in
1781 of consumption aggravated by an incident during the anti-
Catholic Gordon Riots of 1780. Maria commented in later life,
'I was very unlucky.' However, Fitzherbert left her a substantial
income, which allowed her to return to England and take two
houses – one in Mayfair, and the other a delightful Palladian
villa on the banks of the Thames at Twickenham: Marble Hill
House. She entered London society through the front door
and was welcomed into the London Whig circle. Richard
Cosway, the miniaturist, painted her as a shepherdess showing
off her fair curls, dark-brown eyes and delicate complexion,
but she also had a full face with a prominent nose and a long
chin. The feature that particularly appealed to the Prince was
her ample bosom.

The Prince first noticed Maria Fitzherbert at the opera and
he then besieged her passionately. She rejected an offer to
become his mistress and to live in Carlton House; instead
she planned to return to Paris. On hearing of her decision,
in a superb act of melodrama, George stabbed himself and
declared that he would commit suicide unless he could marry
her. Eventually, accompanied by a chaperone, the Duchess of
Devonshire, she went to Carlton House and met the Prince
lying on a couch covered in blood: he begged her to marry him.
She did allow him to put a ring, which he borrowed from the
Duchess of Devonshire, on her finger, and a document was
drawn up. On the following day she left for the Continent and
the Prince bombarded her with passionate letters – one as long
as forty-two pages. She remained abroad for the next year, but
this did not cool George's ardour.

Maria Fitzherbert returned to England after receiving a
letter from the Prince on 3 November 1785 declaring that he
would 'through life endeavour to convince her by his love and
cultivation of his wishes to be the best of husbands.' Could anything be more explicit? They went through a ceremony of
marriage in the drawing room of her house in Park Street,

## Three Weeks After Marriage

1786

WILLIAM DENT

*An alarmed Maria comes across George looking through a list of wives and widows whose pictures Weltje is showing him. 'The originals have been carefully tried and are in fine order for your H—s, as for Fitz she must put up with my comfits, for you know your H—s, you may have twenty such wives.' Maria questions, 'Confusion! Have I been set up with a mock marriage...'? Portraits of Perdita and Mrs Armistead look down upon the scene and a book with the title* Who's the Dupe *falls to the floor. Dent does not beat about the bush – even if there was a marriage it meant nothing.*

Mayfair, on 15 December 1785. The service was conducted by an Anglican clergyman, the Reverend Robert Burt, who had been released from the Fleet Prison with the payment of his debts of £500 and a promise that he would be appointed one of the Prince's chaplains. It was also arranged that Burt would leave the country immediately after the ceremony since it was a capital offence to conduct the marriage service of the heir to the throne without the approval of the King. The service was witnessed by Maria's uncle, Henry Errington, and her brother, John Smythe. The happy couple went off to their honeymoon in a cottage on Ham Common.

In the view of the Catholic Church a marriage had taken place. Fifteen years later Rome declared that the Catholic Mrs Fitzherbert was indeed the wife of the Prince of Wales, and for her this was a marriage in the eyes of God. However, under Anglican Canon Law the position was not quite so clear. There had been no publication of the banns of marriage and the appropriate alternative involving a special licence from the Archbishop of Canterbury, which would have been needed in any event for a legitimate service to be held in a private residence, was not obtained. These omissions certainly made the

marriage irregular but probably did not invalidate it. But, Acts of Parliament are above Anglican Canon Law and the Act of Settlement of 1701 excluded from the throne not only Catholics but also anyone who should 'marry a Papist'. The succession would then pass to the next in line, George's brother and his father's favourite, Frederick, the Duke of York. Furthermore, the Royal Marriages Act of 1772 required the Prince to obtain from King George III his prior consent to any marriage. George III had not been asked to give his consent and therefore under English law the marriage was null and void.

Charles James Fox had strongly advised against this marriage, reminding the Prince that his brother, the Duke of York, would certainly follow his father's wishes as to his bride; that Catholics were still unpopular in the country; and that all this would lead to George forfeiting his right to succeed. Fox also dealt with the possibility that when George became King he could attempt to repeal all Acts against his marriage, and marry Mrs Fitzherbert again. Fox wisely forecast that this subterfuge would not be acceptable to the people, as Mrs Fitzherbert would not be fit to be Queen if she had been living as his mistress in the preceding years. The Prince assured Fox that there 'never was

THE LOVER's LEAP.

Publish'd March 21 1786 by S.W. Fores at the Caracature Warehouse No 3. Piccadilly

**The Lover's Leap**

21 March 1786

HENRY KINGSBURY

*Fox, quite erroneously, is shown encouraging the royal match and he is grotesquely caricatured with his breeches extending up to his neck, indicating that he is a 'Mister Nobody'. The cat is out of the bag and the significance of the broomstick, as one of the carousing companions at the back says, is that it is the instrument with which his father would belabour him. It was also a custom for a bride and groom to jump over a broomstick in order to bring good luck. Fox is shown as being complicit, but he had opposed the marriage.*

any ground for these reports [of the marriage] which of late have been so malevolently circulated.'

The Prince and Maria lived in separate houses: George remained at Carlton House and she rented a house in St James's Square, just round the corner. But the Court gossips soon cottoned on to the fact that something had happened. George never admitted that he had married her but he ensured that the only invitations he accepted were those that included her, and they appeared together at the opera.

On 27 April 1787 there was a motion in the House of Commons to relieve the Prince of all his debts. One MP rose to question whether there was any truth in the rumours of a marriage to a Catholic, which would debar George from inheriting the Crown. It looked as if the motion would not pass. On 30 April Charles James Fox said that George, as a peer of parliament, was ready in the House of Peers to submit to answer any of the most difficult questions that could be put to him. Fox then declared 'with the immediate authority of the Prince of Wales' that the rumoured marriage 'not only never could have happened legally, but never did happen in any way whatsoever.' The motion to pay the debts was passed. But Fox had been

completely misled by the Prince, who avoided meeting him for a whole year. Fox was also dismissed by Maria Fitzherbert, who never spoke to him again, since his speech in Parliament had, in effect, declared her to be the Prince's mistress.

Initially George was delighted, but Maria refused to see him. George persuaded Sheridan to speak in the House of Commons and say some kind words about her. When this failed to work, George once again dramatically took to his bed with a fever inflamed by wine, and threatened to kill himself. The old dodge was effective and Maria returned.

They spent most of the next year together in Brighton. She had an annuity of £2,000 a year and, in the three years when they lived between London and Brighton, she did from time to time pay a little to keep the bailiffs away from her husband. By 1794, however, the Prince had grown tired of her and was infatuated with Anna Maria Crouch, an opera singer. He also had an affair with a young woman called Lucy Howard, who bore him a child. Sheridan hit the nail on the head when he said of George, 'He was too much every lady's man to be the man of any lady.'

George, never at a loss to put the blame on someone else, told his brother Frederick that 'in short we are finally parted,

Defign'd by Carlo Khan    WIFE & no WIFE ____ or ____ A trip to the Continent.    Publifh'd by Will.ᵐ Holland N.º 50 Oxford Str.ᵗ London. March 27 1788

## Wife and No Wife, or, A Trip to the Continent

27 March 1786

JAMES GILLRAY

*This is the most celebrated print of the wedding, but it is a complete fiction. Burke, dressed as usual as a Jesuit, conducts the marriage in a Catholic church; Fox gives the bride away watched by Weltje, the Prince's cook who had become a major-domo; and Hanger looks on. Lord North lies asleep dressed as a coachman, implying a runaway match. The pictures that adorn the church show David watching the bathing Bathsheba, and the one above Fox's head is Judas kissing Christ.*

but parted amicably, and I believe from what you know of my temper, disposition, and the unvaried attention that I have ever treated her with, you will not lay the fault, whatever it may be, at my door.'

George, at this time, had come to believe that he could regularize his relationship through a morganatic marriage to Maria Fitzherbert. Some of his sisters thought this would be a very sensible arrangement but this would have been fraught with difficulty: if George had undertaken any sort of marriage that was valid, then his subsequent union with Caroline of Brunswick – the Princess of Wales – would have been bigamous and Princess Charlotte illegitimate. Caroline later said, 'I never did commit adultery but once and I have repented it ever since. It was with the husband of Mrs Fitzherbert.'

George's attention had now lighted upon Lady Jersey, but after a three-year affair he turned again to Maria. He was distraught on hearing a rumour that she had died but he then received word that they might get together again, but on her terms, which included that she would not live as his mistress or wife, that they should inhabit separate houses, and live as siblings. She would, however, seek a papal blessing for their marriage. In June 1800 she eventually capitulated and gave a great breakfast for him in her house in Tilney Street, London, to let the world know. The following five years were probably the happiest they spent together – her comment was 'we lived like brother and sister.'

There was endless speculation about whether there was a child from this union. Maria Fitzherbert made an affidavit after George's death, though she never signed it, affirming that 'my union with George, Prince of Wales, was without issue.' Despite this, many rumours persisted, particularly surrounding Minnie Seymour, a girl whom Maria was said to have adopted, but many thought was her daughter. But Minnie's parents were traced. Another was Ann Smythe, who had lived with Maria as an adopted daughter and was supposedly the bastard child of her brother. The descendants of Anne Smythe came to believe that George was their blood ancestor.

But George was incapable of being faithful to one woman. He told a friend in the summer of 1808, 'living with one person was like living alone and of that you know one soon grows

HIS HIGHNESS IN FITZ

### His Highness in Fitz

1 April 1786

*There is little caricature in this explicit act of royal fornication. Maria's garter reads 'mal y pense' and George's 'soit'. No previous cartoon had been so explicit and I know of no such cartoon involving a senior member of the Royal Family that has appeared since. This is George's unique record.*

## The Royal Exhibition, or, A Peep at the Marriage Heads

9 May 1786

WILLIAM DENT

*No copy of this print is in the British Museum. It is one of the caricatures in the Royal Collection, which were sold to the Library of Congress in 1921 for the paltry sum of £3,000 so that George V could have more money for his stamp collection. Dent was one of the most frank of the 18th-century cartoonists and he did not mind at all the sheer vulgarity of exposing the bottoms of George and Maria Fitzherbert, with Hanger on the left and Weltje on the right. This is an early demonstration of a practice that in the 20th century came to be called 'mooning'.*

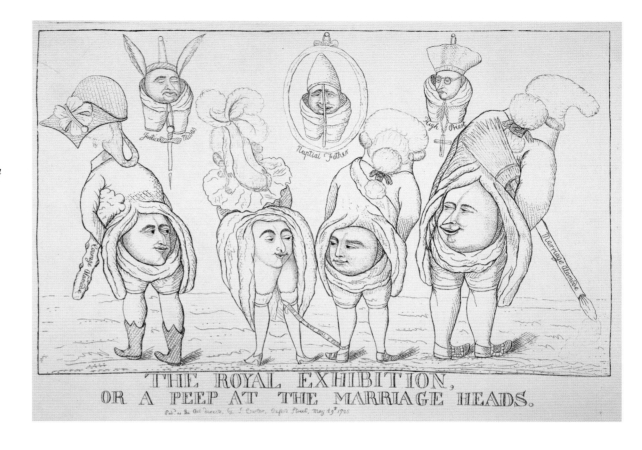

tired.' Maria Fitzherbert had to suffer the introduction in 1806 of yet another favourite, Lady Hertford, but stoically she continued to attend gatherings at Carlton House and at the Pavilion in Brighton. In 1809 she could not stand it any longer – twenty-four years after her marriage she was not prepared to be slighted and wrote a farewell letter to George saying, 'I feel I owe it to myself not to be insulted under your roof with impunity.' Slighted and insulted she behaved with the sort of dignity that her 'husband' could never command.

The final rupture came in the summer of 1811 when George, as Regent, gave a party at Carlton House in honour of the French royal family, honouring as his main guest the Duchesse d'Angoulême. Maria Fitzherbert, then fifty-five, enquired of the Regent whether she would sit at the royal supper table if she attended the dinner. He replied coldly, 'You know, madam, you have no place.' 'None, Sir, but such as you choose to give me.' She refused to go and they never spoke to each other again.

Maria Fitzherbert wrote to her long-standing friend Lady Ann Lindsay in August 1811:

When I reflect upon those happy days many a pang crosses my mind and my heart grows sick at the reflection of the many miseries and persecutions I have suffered since that period all occasioned by the man for whom I have sacrificed everything and who never hesitates to sacrifice me to gratify every caprice that comes into his head and who is, I feel, a total stranger to principle or honour.

However, there were some consolations for Maria. From 1815 Brighton became her main residence, where she was looked upon as a celebrity, so much so that when George went to Brighton he rarely stirred from the Pavilion – her sweet revenge. Her annuity of £6,000 was continued and on his death increased to £10,000 (£600,000 in today's money).

Maria Fitzherbert was the only one of George's paramours who really cared for him, who showed him affection, who helped him out financially, who fiercely defended his reputation, and was prepared to put herself in an impossible legal position, which she fully recognized, because of her love for him. George

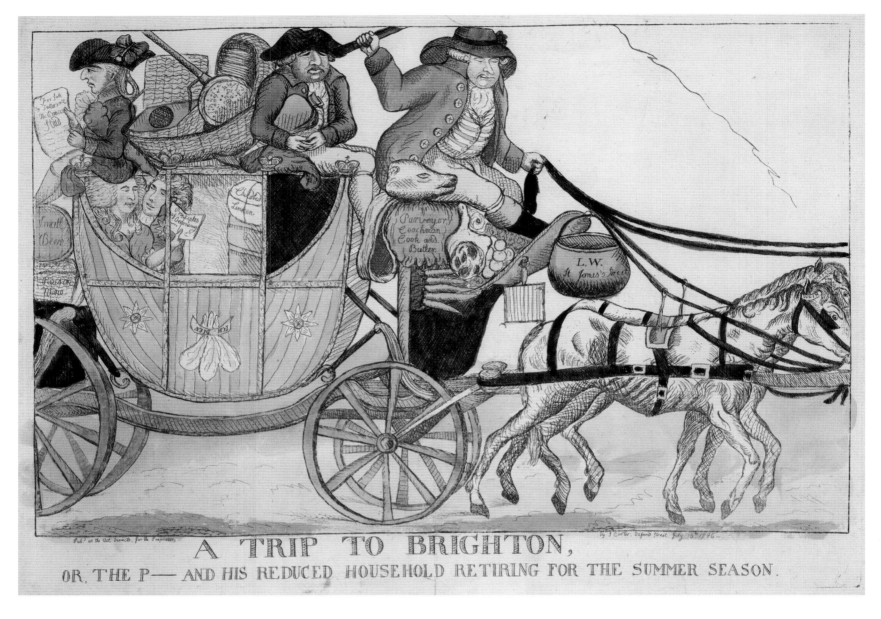

A TRIP TO BRIGHTON,
OR, THE P—— AND HIS REDUCED HOUSEHOLD RETIRING FOR THE SUMMER SEASON.

**A Trip to Brighton, or, The P——
and his Reduced Household
Retiring for the Summer Season**

15 July 1786

WILLIAM DENT

*Principally to embarrass George III, the Prince ostentatiously
cut back his spending – closing Carlton House and moving
to Brighton. 'Purveyor, Coachman, Cook and Butler' Weltje
drives the coach, with Hanger and Fox on top. Mrs Fitzherbert
reads* Principles of Oeconomy *while George gazes at her
besottedly. Inside the coach there is a box labelled 'Child Bed
Linen' and on top there is a cradle. It was widely believed that
Mrs Fitzherbert was pregnant. The print's date is exactly seven
months after her marriage.*

threw all this away on a series of mistresses who became steadily more grotesque and each of whom fed on his fame, fortune and position to enhance her own and her family's position in society. As a fickle philanderer consumed with his own vanity, devoted only to those things that could give him pleasure, he reaped where he had sown.

When it became known that George was slowly dying, Maria Fitzherbert, who had not seen her former lover for many years, wrote to him saying:

> After many repeated struggles with myself and the apprehension of appearing troublesome and intruding upon your Majesty after so many years of continued silence, my anxiety respecting your Majesty has got the better of my

THE KINGS EVIL.

Pub.d by S.W. Fores Sept.t 28 1786 at the caricature warehouse no. 3 Piccadilly.

## The —— [Prince's] Nursery, or, Nine Months After —— [Marriage]

9 May 1786

*This speculates on the implications of a child resulting from George and Maria's marriage. In the picture on the wall, a bishop is christening a baby. The little boy wearing a papal hat is a reminder that any child would have to be brought up a Catholic. There were many rumours that Maria Fitzherbert had a child. Later in her life she prepared a document that ended with the statement: 'I, Maria Fitzherbert, moreover testify that my union with George, Prince of Wales, was without issue.' But she did not sign it in the space provided.*

## The King's Evil

28 September 1786

*This is a more explicit print. Mrs Fitzherbert spreads her legs immodestly and the Garter ribbon bears the phrase 'Evil to them that evil think.' The objects on the table suggest a venereal infection. There is a hint that the Prince is already tired of his impetuous love.*

DIDO FORSAKEN. Sic transit gloria Reginæ.

Pub.d Mar.21.st.1787. by. S.W.Fores, Piccadilly, London.

## Dido Forsaken. Sic Transit Gloria Reginae

2 June 1787

JAMES GILLRAY

*This is a satire on Fox's declaration, during the debate on the Prince's debts, that there was no marriage. Pitt and his colleague Dundas, who had gone to Carlton House to do a deal with the Prince, are blowing the crown, orb and sceptre off Maria Fitzherbert's head. Another wind blows away a boat carrying Fox, Burke and the Prince, who is saying, 'I never saw her in my life.' Lying at her feet are symbols of Catholicism – a sharp-toothed harrow 'for the conversion of heretics'; a scourge; a rosary; and a crucifix. The mound on which Maria sits appears at first sight to be made of moneybags, but closer inspection reveals them to be penises.*

## George Shackled

3 April 1788

*The following year George submits to the 'Delightful Slavery' of Maria Fitzherbert, who says, 'Who can behold without transport "the glass of fashion and the mould of form, the observ'd of all observers" smiling in chains.'*

scruples and I trust your Majesty will believe me most sincere when I assure you how truly I have grieved to hear of your sufferings....No one will feel more rejoiced to learn your Majesty is restored to complete convalescence.

George did not reply, but he put the letter under his pillow. After his death, a locket was found hung around his neck containing the miniature portrait of Maria by Cosway.

THE NEW BIRTH

Pub. Dec 17.1789 by S.W.Fores at his Caricatura Exhibition Rooms Nº 3 Piccadilly The Compleatest Collection in the Kingdom Admit. 1 Shilling

**The New Birth**

17 December 1789

ISAAC CRUIKSHANK

*Rumours of Maria's pregnancy persisted, and produced a spate of prints implying that a child had been born. This one emphasizes the Catholic element: a priest is at hand to baptise the child, who is brought in a warming pan – the very device used to disguise the birth of James II's son in 1689, which, had he been discovered, would have ensured a Catholic succession.*

A BLACK JOKE.

**A Black Joke**

24 October 1790

*This unusual and rare print shows George, Maria and Fox playing cards. George and Maria have failed to take a trick and Fox has taken all three, probably helped by his hand beneath the table. The meaning is rather obscure as Maria never spoke to Fox after his denial in the House of Commons of the marriage. This striking image was inspired by a coarse song, The Black Joke – slang for the female pudenda.*

# 8 The Miserable Husband

CAROLINE OF BRUNSWICK was born in 1768. Her mother, Augusta, was the eldest sister of George III. So, when George married Caroline he was keeping it in the family by marrying a first cousin. She was almost betrothed on two prior occasions and there was an unsubstantiated rumour that at the age of fifteen she had to have an abortion. In 1794 Caroline started to learn English. George told his father that provided his debts were paid he would agree to marry the Princess of Brunswick. Wellington much later told Lady Salisbury, 'Lady Jersey made the marriage simply because she wished to put Mrs Fitzherbert on the same footing as herself and deprive her of the claim of lawful wife.'

The main advantage to George was that Parliament would increase his income from £60,000 a year to £100,000 on his marriage. As a lampoon put it:

> …The prince he said, 'Good father, if you will find
> the money,
> You may send for which you please, and she shall be
> my honey.
> There's Caroline of Brunswick has got a pretty hand, sir.
> Do you but pay my debts, and I'll take it at command, sir.'

In November 1794 Lord Malmesbury went to Brunswick to meet the Princess and initiate the marriage proceedings. Much of our knowledge of her character and behaviour comes from the diaries he kept. On 20 November he recorded his first impression: 'A pretty face – not expressive of softness – a figure not graceful – fine eyes – good hand – tolerable teeth but going – fair hair and light eyebrows – good bust – short.' She was twenty-six. Malmesbury signed the marriage treaty. He learnt from her father that Caroline had a habit of giving her opinions aloud; she had no tact and she was not very clever.

The departure for England, accompanied by Malmesbury, was delayed for over two months by the war in the Netherlands. While they were waiting, Malmesbury on two occasions complained to Caroline about her lack of personal cleanliness. In fact she frequently stank. 'She seldom washed her hair or feet, and she wore coarse petticoats, coarse shifts, and thread stockings, which were never well washed or changed enough,' he confided to his diary.

George had insisted that Caroline's lady-in-waiting should be his mistress, Lady Jersey, who accordingly greeted the Princess when she arrived in England on 3 April 1795. Caroline met the Prince at St James's Palace on 5 April. Lord Malmesbury confided in his diary, 'She very properly, in consequence of my saying to her it was the right mode of proceeding, attempted to kneel to him. He raised her (gracefully enough), and embraced her, said barely one word, turned round, retired to a distant part of the apartment, and calling me to him said, "Harris, I am not well; pray get me a glass of brandy."' At the dinner later that evening Caroline was flippant and threw out coarse, vulgar hints about Lady Jersey that compounded the Prince's disgust. The following day it got worse when Caroline, not unnaturally, complained of Lady Jersey and challenged her future husband about the relationship. Although they had exchanged miniatures of themselves they were both disappointed with the other's appearance. George was fastidious in his clothes, his manners and his life. He did not want a wife who smelt.

George and Caroline married on the evening of Wednesday, 8 April 1795 in the Chapel Royal, St James's Palace. On the morning of his wedding George said to his brother the Duke of

## The Lover's Dream

24 January 1795

JAMES GILLRAY

*This is a deeply ironic print, since Caroline had not set foot in England and the full ghastliness of what was about to occur could not be foreseen by Gillray (though he does hint that not all will be well). Caroline, assisted by Hymen carrying a torch, hovers over the dreaming Prince while Cupid pulls aside the bed's heavy curtains. A gleeful George III is happy to pay off his son's debts and the Queen holds a book on childbirth. However, Fox is so worried that he drops the dice from his dicebox; Sheridan slinks away disguised as a Jew, while Derby falls off a cask of port; and Mrs Fitzherbert and Lady Jersey know their days are over. The Prince is clearly prepared for marital bliss as a chamberpot holds a bottle to cure the pox.*

The LOVER'S DREAM.

"A Thousand Virtues seem to lackey her, Driving far off each thing of Sin & Guilt." Milton.

J.ˢ Gillray des.ⁿ et fect.

Pub.ᵈ Jan.ʸ 24ᵗʰ 1795. by H.Humphry N.º 87. New Bond Street.

97

OH! CHE BOCCONE!

## Oh! Che Boccone!

15 April 1795

ISAAC CRUIKSHANK

*Oh! What a mouthful! This is the first print to comment on the marriage, which had taken place the previous week. Stories of the doomed relationship must have been slipping out, for Caroline, who smiles alluringly, cannot tempt her husband into the wedding bed.*

*George, always keen to justify what he did, told Malmesbury that he had sexual relations with her on three nights but that 'she showed such marks of filth both in the fore and hind part of her…that she turned my stomach.'*

*Lady Charlotte Campbell recorded in her diary Caroline's comment on her wedding night: 'Judge what it was to have a drunken husband on one's wedding day, one who had passed the greatest part of his bridal night under the grate where he fell and where I left him.' It is likely that a child was conceived around 16 April; Caroline later said that they had ceased to live as man and wife only two or three weeks after marriage, and she hinted at George's impotence.*

*George could not face the indignity of knowing that she found him inadequate and he confided to a friend that Caroline in her moment of passion declared, 'Ah, mon dieu, qu'il est gros!'*

Clarence, 'William, tell Mrs Fitzherbert she is the only woman I shall ever love.' As he walked up the aisle he was quite drunk and had to be held up by the Dukes of Bedford and Roxburghe.

Within a few weeks Caroline and George could barely stand being with each other and in September the Prince told his mother that the Princess was 'as wicked, as slanderous, as lying, as ever'. At one dinner when George drank from Lady Jersey's glass, Caroline snatched a guest's pipe and puffed it contemptuously at her husband. The chattering classes at the London Court certainly knew of the coolness between the Prince and Princess of Wales, and the role that Lady Jersey had played in it.

Caroline gave birth to a daughter on 7 January 1796 – 'an immense girl'. The King hoped that the new baby would be 'a bond of additional union' between Caroline and George. He could not have been more wrong. Within a few days of the birth George wrote a will and testament, running to over three thousand words, in which he left the Princess of Wales one shilling and assigned his daughter, Charlotte, to the care of his father and mother. George's will was to give

all my worldly property of every description to my Maria Fitzherbert…the wife of my heart and soul and though by the laws of this country she could not have made herself public in that name, still such as is it in the eyes of Heaven, was and is and ever will be such in mine.

He left her everything: the entire contents of Carlton House, his books, jewels, watches, horses, carriages and the property in Brighton. This will, however, was never witnessed, and Lady Jersey soon reasserted her fascination over him.

George was embarrassed by his wife. In a series of letters he begged Caroline to accept that they should not live together and should, in effect, separate: 'Nature has not made us suitable to each other.' He asked his father for a separation, but George III firmly declined this. To his friends George was even more explicit about Caroline – 'a very master of iniquity'; 'an infamous wretch'; there was 'no end to her wickedness…and her designs.' He was determined to get rid of Caroline. Rumours of her scandalous behaviour at parties in her house at Blackheath later gave him a chance to secure her expulsion.

**Future Prospects, or, Symptoms of Love in High Life**

31 May 1796

*It was clear by the end of May that the marriage was at its end. Here George, in a tantrum, declares, 'Marriage has no restraints on me! No legal tie can bind the will' – a statement that requires no further explanation, as the cuckold Lord Jersey tells him that his wife, with her legs wide open, is waiting for him on the bed next door.*

The PRESENTATION ____ or ____ The Wise Men's Offering.

**The Presentation, or, The Wise Men's Offering**

9 January 1796

JAMES GILLRAY

*Princess Charlotte had been born two days before this print appeared and here she is welcomed by her drunken and dishevelled father. Two of the 'wise men' are Fox and Sheridan, ingratiating themselves with the next generation. Caroline, who never lost an opportunity to denigrate her husband, told an acquaintance that when she revealed her pregnancy to George he announced that the child was not his. This print became famous as Gillray was pursued through the Ecclesiastical Court on the grounds of blasphemy.*

ENCHANTMENTS *lately seen upon the* Mountains *of* WALES, — *or* — Shon-ap-Morgan's Reconcilement *to the Fairy Princess.*

## Enchantments Lately Seen Upon the Mountains of Wales, or, Shon–ap–Morgan's Reconcilement to the Fairy Princess

30 June 1796

JAMES GILLRAY

*George saw more of Lady Jersey than he did of his wife and he may well have been the father of a boy she produced in the autumn of 1795. By March 1796 George had decided upon a separation, which was denied by his father. Lady Jersey overplayed her hand and the King insisted in June that she should leave the Prince's household. The* London Chronicle *reported that the Princess had dined at Carlton House and there was a prospect of reconciliation, but the next day George met Lady Jersey in Brighton and they spent a dirty weekend together at Bognor. Caroline had only contempt for George: on attending an opera at which she was cheered, Caroline was warned of the threat of assassins, but she commented, 'When the daughter of a hero marries a zero, she doesn't fear gunfire.'*

# 9 The Family

MONSTROUS CRAWS, at a New Coalition Feast.

**Monstrous Craws at a New Coalition Feast**

29 May 1787

JAMES GILLRAY

*In the 18th century people seen as freaks were put on show. Three people with large goitres were exhibited in London as 'wild-born human beings'.*

*Here George III, on the right, Queen Charlotte, depicted as a hag, and the Prince of Wales barely caricatured but wearing a fool's cap, are stuffing ladlefuls of guineas into large pouches in their throats. The Prince's pouch is empty. After two years of arguing with his father the Prince's debts had been settled by Parliament the month this print appeared. It reflects George's quasi-reconciliation with his parents, which was short-lived as George had to be bailed out again in 1795 and 1802.*

THE RELATIONSHIPS between the fathers and sons of the House of Hanover were strained and distant, saturated with suspicion and jealousy, swinging capriciously from spurts of generosity to improving lectures. This led to feelings of insolent frustration on part of Hanoverian sons and aggrieved betrayal on that of the fathers.

George III was what would be called today a control freak. He tried to control his governments, though he was ill-equipped to do so, and he actively encouraged them to control the American colonies – a task that was geographically, militarily, socially and economically impossible. After the Battle of Lexington, he said 'once these rebels have felt a smart blow they will submit.' It led to the greatest humiliation of his reign. He applied the same frenetic desire to control everything to his family, with similarly disastrous results. His daughters had to live with their parents in Buckingham House and Windsor in an establishment that they called 'The Nunnery'. They were not allowed to marry the men they wanted. All the King's sons resented his continual interference: they rebelled against the regime he tried to foist upon them and decided to lead their own dissolute lives. His relationship with his heir, the Prince of Wales, was the most intense for he both loved and hated him. He gave him no training in the affairs of state; he denied him any public role; and he was openly critical of him to his ministers.

Detecting in his eldest son at the early age of twelve one of the characteristics that was to prevail throughout the boy's life, George III complained to one of his tutors that the Prince of Wales had 'a bad habit of not speaking the truth'. By the age of sixteen, his father knew, he was keeping loose company; had fallen in love with Mary Hamilton; went frequently to the theatre; and was about to have an affair with Mary 'Perdita' Robinson, the celebrated actress. Within a year the King would have to approach the Prime Minister, Lord North, for £5,000 to pay her off.

The King insisted that when George reached the age of eighteen he should live in Buckingham House; that he should dine there at least two evenings a week; attend his mother's drawing rooms; decline invitations to private parties; and never go to a masquerade. In addition, whenever the King was to go out riding the Prince was to accompany him. George showed

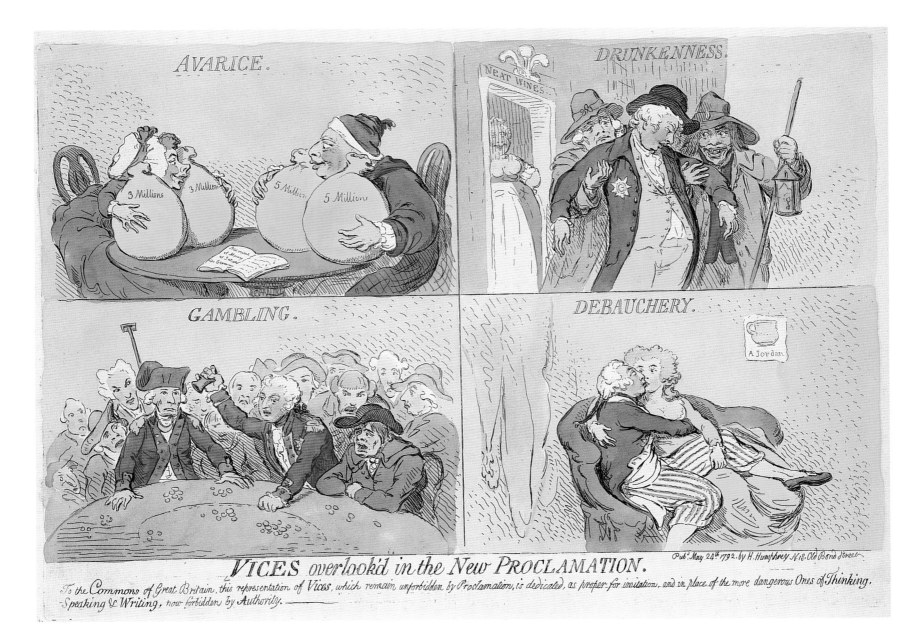

## Vices Overlook'd in the New Proclamation

24 May 1792

JAMES GILLRAY

The Royal Proclamation of 21 May for 'the preventing of tumultuous meetings and seditious writings' was a panic reaction to the fear that there would be widespread rioting in support of Thomas Paine's revolutionary writings. It was attacked by Grey and the Whigs, though supported by the Prince of Wales in his maiden speech in the House of Lords, which led to a break with Fox. Gillray could not resist the contrast between the liberties being taken away from the people and the indulgence given to the royal family, who were left free to engage in their vices. George III and Charlotte hoard money as misers; the Duke of York gambles; the Duke of Clarence embraces his mistress Mrs Jordan; and the Prince of Wales staggers drunkenly from a bawdy house to be taken home by the nightwatch.

The RECONCILIATION. ([And he arose and came to his Father, and his Father saw him, & had compassion, & ran, & fell on his Neck, & kissed him. Read the Parable. Verse 16th. to 24th.

## The Reconciliation

20 November 1804

JAMES GILLRAY

*Pressed by Pitt and Lord Chancellor Eldon in the spring of 1804, George was prepared for a public reconciliation with his father. The meeting was postponed because the King had made some favourable remarks about the Princess of Wales. Father and son met at last at Kew on 20 November in the presence of the Queen and some of George's sisters. To celebrate, Gillray took the lines from the return of the Prodigal Son.*

little respect for his father. His brother the Duke of York revealed much later to his mistress, Mrs Clarke, that 'When an interview took place between them, the Prince used to stand up to His Majesty with his hands in his pockets.' In his letters to his son George III was openly critical:

> The Prince of Wales on the smallest reflection must feel that I have little reason to approve of any part of his conduct for the last three years; that his neglect of every religious duty is notorious; his want of common civility to the Queen and me, not less so; besides his total disobedience of every injunction I have given and which he in the presence of his brothers and the gentlemen about them both declared himself contented with. I must hope he will now think it behoves him to take a fresh line of conduct worthy of his station.

Those words fell on barren ground. The Prince had no intention of changing his lifestyle.

A SEPULCHRAL ENQUIRY into ENGLISH HISTORY.

The central cause of the sourness in the relationship was the King's refusal to settle his son's debts. George III had only modest personal wealth from which he had to sustain a large family of unmarried daughters and sons. The extravagant and unstoppable lifestyle of his eldest son soon ran up debts of £150,000 (£14 million in today's money) a sum the King simply did not have. The King also knew that this would not be the end of it. The Prince took this refusal as a personal insult and in 1784 he remarked to Sir James Harris, HM Minister at the Hague, who was later ennobled as the Earl of Malmesbury and acted as the intermediary with Caroline of Brunswick, 'What, my dear Harris, will you force me to repeat to you that *the King hates me?* He will never be reconciled to me….He wishes me dead – ruin'd – that I should appear contemptible in the eyes of the world.'

George III was trying to fashion in his heir a pattern of correct behaviour, but he did not appreciate that his son had

## A Sepulchral Enquiry into English History

1 June 1813

GEORGE CRUIKSHANK

*This print appeared in the* Scourge. *In April, the coffins of Charles I and Henry VIII at St George's Chapel, Windsor had been opened in the presence of George and the Duke of Cumberland. Charles I's head was identified but Henry VIII's coffin held only a skeleton with a trace of a beard. There were several squibs about this, relating George's behaviour to that of his two predecessors: 'Charles to his people, Henry to his wife.' McMahon, the Regent's Private Secretary, observes that they should take a tip from Henry VIII, who had a way of dealing with his wives. Sir Henry Halford, the royal physician, holds Charles I's head. As a memento, he took a cervical vertebra of Charles I that had been cut through by the executioner's axe – he liked to pass this around at his dinner table.*

simply nothing to do. There were no good works to take up, no official visits to make, no campaigns to plan, no exotic tours of foreign countries. The Prince just had to fill each day as well as he could and, being surrounded by flatterers, wastrels, cadgers and all those who hoped to gain favour by being in the Prince of Wales's circle, it is not surprising that he spent many hours in the company of tailors, shoemakers, hosiers, hatters, jewellers, cabinet-makers, art dealers and racing cronies. His retorts to his father's rebukes were to say that he had always found the day was long enough for doing nothing.

George always showed great affection to his sisters, who suffered even more in the bosom of the family than he did. George III and Queen Charlotte imposed upon their daughters impossibly restrictive conditions. They were not allowed to marry members of any English noble families; only continental princes were considered suitable. Princess Charlotte, the eldest, was eventually allowed to marry the immensely fat Duke of Württemberg when she was thirty-one; Augusta may have been secretly married; Elizabeth had two or three children and she was eventually married at the age of forty-seven to the similarly obese Landgrave of Hesse-Homburg; Mary married, aged forty, her cousin the Duke of Gloucester; Sophia gave birth to a son in 1800 who there is good reason to believe was fathered by her brother Ernest, the Duke of Cumberland.

George's relationship with his brothers ebbed and flowed. In youth he was closest to Frederick, Duke of York, but became jealous when Frederick was made commander-in-chief of the army. However, after Frederick fell from grace for jobbery, George – as his first act as Regent – reappointed him. Frederick failed to produce an heir. William, his second brother, played little part in George's life and was only important when he became the heir to the throne. The Duke of Cumberland was the most gruesome of the band – aside from the rumours about Sophia he was an extreme and violent reactionary who murdered his valet. Later he plotted and intrigued against his brother, chiefly to prevent Catholic emancipation.

They were a dysfunctional family. The seven sons of George III (he had nine but two died in early infancy) produced only two legitimate heirs but between them they had eighteen illegitimate children. When Creevey told Wellington that there were proposals to increase the money for the establishment of the royal dukes, the Iron Duke pungently commented,

They are the damndest millstone about the necks of any government that can be imagined. They have insulted – personally insulted – two-thirds of the gentlemen of England and how can it be wondered that they take their revenge upon them when they get them in the House of Commons. It is their only opportunity, and I think, by God, they are quite right to use it.

JOHN BULL IN THE COUNCIL CHAMBER

## John Bull in the Council Chamber

1 July 1813

GEORGE CRUIKSHANK

*This is a malevolent satire on the unpopular, dysfunctional royal family, produced during the second inquiry into Caroline's conduct. Halford, on the extreme left, carries reports on the King's health; Canning, appearing in scales, declares that the Princess of Wales is innocent – news not welcomed by the Queen, who declares that she will preserve her prerogative.*

*As a raddled snuff addict – 'Old Snuffy' – the Queen is offered her favourite Royal Strasburgh by three courtiers and three imps, while two snakes protect her moneybags. Her skinny foot rests on a footstool containing the Hastings diamond; the Queen's love of jewels earned her the title 'Queen of Diamonds'. When she died in 1818 it was estimated that her jewels alone were worth £200,000 (£9 million in today's money). Meanwhile, the Regent is a baby fondling a Lady Hertford doll and is provided with a bottle of curaçao. An amazed and puzzled John Bull despairs of 'Conscience asleep!'*

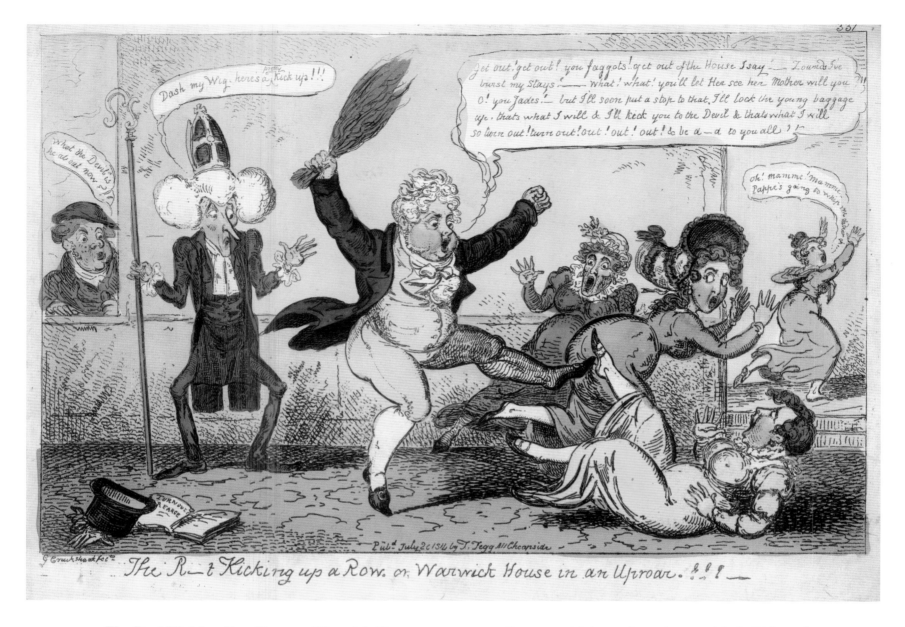

## The R—t Kicking Up a Row, or, Warwick House in an Uproar!

20 July 1814

GEORGE CRUIKSHANK

*This incident in George's attempts to control his unruly daughter revealed that he had learnt nothing from the way he had been treated by his father. Charlotte had broken off her engagement to the Prince of Orange without telling her father, who then summoned her to Carlton House. She, in turn, asked*

*George to visit her and, turning up with the Bishop of Salisbury, he told her that her household would be dismissed and she would come under his protection at Carlton House and Windsor. 'I'll lock the young baggage up, that's what I will & I'll kick you to the Devil.' Charlotte slipped out and took a hackney carriage to her mother's house. During the night there were frantic negotiations involving the Duke of York and Brougham for the Princess and Lord Eldon for the Regent, and she was finally persuaded to return. Nonetheless Charlotte had won – she was clearly going to marry whomever she wanted.*

**A German Present, or, The Lover's Token**

April 1816

WILLIAMS

*Charlotte had decided to marry Prince Leopold of Saxe-Coburg-Saalfeld – a handsome, penniless soldier. All he can bring her is a German sausage, and in praise of this phallic offering he says, 'Dat is vat de Yarmany ladies love so vel!' And the décolleté Charlotte replies, 'Oh dear me, it is the longest and thickest I ever saw, do let me taste it.' Her father's experienced advice is, 'You must not take too much of it at a time, you'll find it very hot.'*

ICH DIEN.

Manufactures of Great Britain.

Pub.d by R. Dighton Spring Gardens March 5 1813.

Paternal Protection.

Princess Charlotte had a lot of her mother in her. She was something of a hoyden – blowsy, talkative, rowdy and wilful. Her father described her once as 'stiff-necked, stubborn, and silly'. In fact, by her teens, through hard experience, she had become pretty astute – and amusing. Her mother's influence on her upbringing had been steadily reduced and her father spent his time writing letters to her, changing her companions and staff to exclude any wild or wayward influences. At the age of sixteen she confessed to flirting with a certain Captain Hesse, and it may have gone further, as her mother locked them in a bedroom with the advice, 'Amusez-vous.'

At eighteen Charlotte was persuaded by her father to become engaged to the Prince of Orange – a sallow, dull youth known for his drunkenness. When Charlotte discovered that on marrying the heir to the Dutch throne she would be expected to spend much of her time in Holland, she rebelled, bolstered by advice from Henry Brougham, the radical lawyer and Whig MP to whom controversy came naturally. Her father, her Uncle Frederick, and the Prime Minister Lord Liverpool all tried to persuade her but she firmly refused to go ahead with the marriage. Then she decided to do a bunk. She went to Charing Cross and took a hackney coach to her mother's house in Connaught Place (though Caroline was at Blackheath). While Charlotte was there, Brougham drew up a document clearly stating that she would not marry the Prince of Orange. Various messengers were sent by the Regent to persuade her to come back, and when eventually she took that advice her father promptly dispatched her to a lodge in Windsor Forest, where she was in effect put under house arrest. George drew up a list of people that she was allowed to see and he told her that if she went to the theatre she was not to sit in the front of the box and must leave before the end: he feared a demonstration in her favour. George had learnt nothing from the way that he had been treated by his own father. He sought to impose upon his daughter a similar regime of regulation, against which he had himself rebelled.

## Paternal Protection

*c.* 1814–15

ROBERT DIGHTON

*Only Dighton could be counted on to create the sort of vision that the Prince had of himself, which was not shared by the country.*

Charlotte did, however, meet a suitable suitor: Prince Leopold of Saxe-Coburg-Saalfeld. He was handsome, charming, attentive and well turned-out, and had served as a cavalry officer in the Russian army campaigning against Napoleon. But he was penniless – having to rent apartments above a grocery shop in Marylebone High Street whenever he stayed in London. The prints made great play of this and he is shown wearing ragged clothes, with no breeches, in need of delousing, carrying a large sausage which is clearly phallic, and being treated by his future father-in-law for venereal disease, a subject in which George was an expert.

As Charlotte had decided that Leopold was the best of a poor bunch, George eventually agreed by welcoming them to Brighton and four months later, on 2 May 1816, they were married at Carlton House. Charlotte's allowance was increased by Parliament to £60,000 a year (£3.7 million in today's money) and she received a further £60,000 for furniture, plate and jewels. A rich MP bought Claremont Lodge at Esher and gave it to the royal couple as their home. Leopold had done rather well and it was reported that during the marriage service when he said, 'With all my worldly goods I thee endow,' the bride laughed. He was to do even better, for Leopold ended up as King of the Belgians.

Charlotte was soon pregnant and on 3 November 1817 she started a long labour that lasted for fifty hours – she gave birth to a large boy, but he was stillborn. Charlotte seemed fine at first but a few hours later complained of stomach pains, a singing in her head, and a tightness in her chest. She went into a fit and died. She had suffered a post-partum haemorrhage, but the latest research into the incidence of porphyria in the royal family seems to indicate that she, too, suffered from that hereditary disease. Her obstetrician, Sir Richard Croft, was widely blamed for not using instruments during labour and two years later, when he was attending a similar confinement, he shot himself.

George was devastated by the death of his daughter and relapsed into one of his fits of depression. Charlotte's death shocked the public and a great wave of sympathy swept over the country. Mourning cups, saucers and plates were issued in their hundreds of thousands to commemorate the princess, who many had thought was the brightest hope for the House of Hanover. This was not a view shared by Wellington. He is reported as saying, 'Her death was a blessing to the country,' for she 'would have turned out quite as bad as her mother.'

**A Brighton Hot Bath, or, Preparations for the Wedding!**

April 1816

GEORGE CRUIKSHANK

Prince Leopold was not only poor but alleged to be verminous, flea-ridden and diseased. The Queen delights in pouring scalding water on his private parts, which are being scrubbed by the Lord Chancellor, Eldon. George pours essence of roses into Leopold's mouth to cope with his stinking breath. The phallic German sausage is on the floor together with Ovid's Acts of Love. The scene is watched over by Mercury – the cure for the pox – and George recalls that he 'was served this way myself some twenty years ago'.

## Progeny in Perspective, or, A Royal Accouchment!

1 August 1816

GEORGE CRUIKSHANK

*This is a much happier print. Cruikshank anticipates that Princess Charlotte will have a boy whom the Prince Regent – uncaricatured – proudly shows to his ministers Castlereagh, Eldon and Liverpool. 'See! My Lords a bouncing boy – all square & above board not a bit of trick throughout the business – a fine bouncing boy you see!' The baby directs a stream of urine over the ministers while Queen Charlotte, as a witch, prepares caudle, a drink distributed to celebrate a royal birth. Leopold dances with joy and promises more offspring – a grumpy John Bull fears the boy might be the first of twelve, each costing £6,000 a year. A similar print appeared early in Victoria's reign after the birth of her third child, in which John Bull deplores her fecundity: she had nine children. George, tragically, had only one legitimate grandchild, who died at birth and was shortly followed by his mother.*

**Sales by Auction! or, Provident Children Disposing of Their Deceased Mother's Effects for the Benefit of the Creditors!**

6 May 1819

GEORGE CRUIKSHANK

On the Queen's death George moved quickly to get hold of her jewels, but the rest of her property was sold at auctions by Christie's, between May and August. Her clothes, furniture and famous snuff all went under the hammer, and George, as auctioneer, is urging the buyers, 'So pray my good people bid liberally, or the children will be destitute!' The proceeds of this sale of royal loot would go not to the state but to the family. Lots include the famous ivory bed from India given to the Queen by Mrs Hastings, and Indian clothes which have never been worn and are moth-eaten.

**Fracas Royal Extraordinaire**

August 1820

ISAAC CRUIKSHANK

*Frederick, Duke of York, feared that the divorce process in 1820 would rebound against the monarchy and even affect his position as heir presumptive. This is an imaginary scene but it reveals the tension between the brothers and George's fear that the regiments of the army for which Frederick was responsible could well mutiny in favour of the Queen.*

# 10  The Wayward Wife

THE 'DELICATE INVESTIGATION' was a kangaroo court set up by George III in 1806, at the prompting of the Prince of Wales, to investigate allegations made by Lady Douglas, who had been a close friend and confidante of the Princess of Wales when she was living at Blackheath. Lady Douglas alleged that Caroline had taken lovers and had told her she was pregnant and that Willie Austin, who Caroline claimed was a Deptford boy she had adopted, was in fact her son.

The four peers who were appointed commissioners took evidence from the Douglases and a number of neighbours and servants. Caroline's main lover was thought to be Sir Sidney Smith, a colourful admiral who had shot to fame in 1799 when he had stopped Napoleon's march from Egypt through Syria at the siege of Acre, seizing the French artillery and eighteen French gunboats. He was very conceited, vain, underemployed and overactive. It is likely that he did sleep with Caroline, but no one who had accepted this rather open invitation was going to admit it, for committing adultery with the Princess of Wales was an act of high treason, carrying with it the death penalty.

Another lover was said to be a Captain Thomas Manby, whose career she had tried to promote. After his death, many years later, his brother revealed that Manby had been offered £40,000 to admit to adultery, a bribe that he had turned down. This incident shows the lengths to which George and his agents were prepared to go to find evidence that might lead to a divorce.

The commissioners were soon convinced that Willie Austin was not Caroline's son, as she produced a couple who swore that they were his true parents. But many continued to believe the contrary, and an old gossip, Lord Glenbervie, recalled a dinner in 1807 at which Caroline, noticing Willie in the room, said twice, 'It is a long time since I brought you to bed Willie.' It was clear that much of Lady Douglas's evidence was a malignant fabrication driven by the suspicion that Sidney Smith was enjoying Caroline's favours. The commissioners found Caroline not guilty but they added a rider: 'Other particulars respecting the conduct of Her Royal Highness…considering her exalted rank and station, have necessarily given occasion to very unfavourable interpretation.'

This was a travesty of British justice. The commissioners pretended to be a court, requiring evidence to be given on oath, but the accused was never told that the commission had been appointed; nor what the charges against her were; nor who were the witnesses; and Caroline was given the chance neither to challenge the evidence nor to appear in her own defence. Of course her behaviour at Blackheath had outraged many people. She was vulgar, boisterous and bawdy, and the evidence of a footman at Montague House, Samuel Roberts, was perhaps the most eloquent: 'The Princess is very fond of fucking.'

The commission had been appointed by a Whig government, and so it was not surprising that the Tories, led by Spencer Perceval, took up Caroline's cause. Perceval actively helped her to prepare a pamphlet that came to be known as *The Book*, which was supposed to list the King's adulteries and put a Caroline spin on the Delicate Investigation. It was clearly a reciprocal act and *The Book* was printed but not distributed. When the Tories returned to office Perceval burnt five hundred copies, but his involvement gave him some hold over George and in 1811, when George had been confirmed as Regent and it was thought he would dismiss Perceval in favour of the Whigs, Perceval remained in office. Some prints hinted that this was due to his knowledge of the contents of *The Book*. The Whigs, now out of office, seized upon *The Book* and published it.

Caroline also dabbled in politics. She liked the Whigs when the Tories were in power and vice versa, always hoping that her friends in Opposition would side with her when in office. Like many who harbour such expectations, she was disappointed. But from 1808 she came to depend more and more upon the legal advice of Henry Brougham, whose ambitions were to get into the House of Commons and to receive the silk gown of a King's Counsel.

George and Caroline quarrelled incessantly over how their daughter Charlotte should be brought up. George III intervened and restricted the number of times that Caroline could see her. Brougham, ever ready to stir up trouble with the Prince, advised Caroline to see her daughter whenever she wanted. This made George even more determined to limit Caroline's influence, particularly as she acquired a string of new lovers, including Lord Henry FitzGerald and an Italian musician, Pietro Sapio.

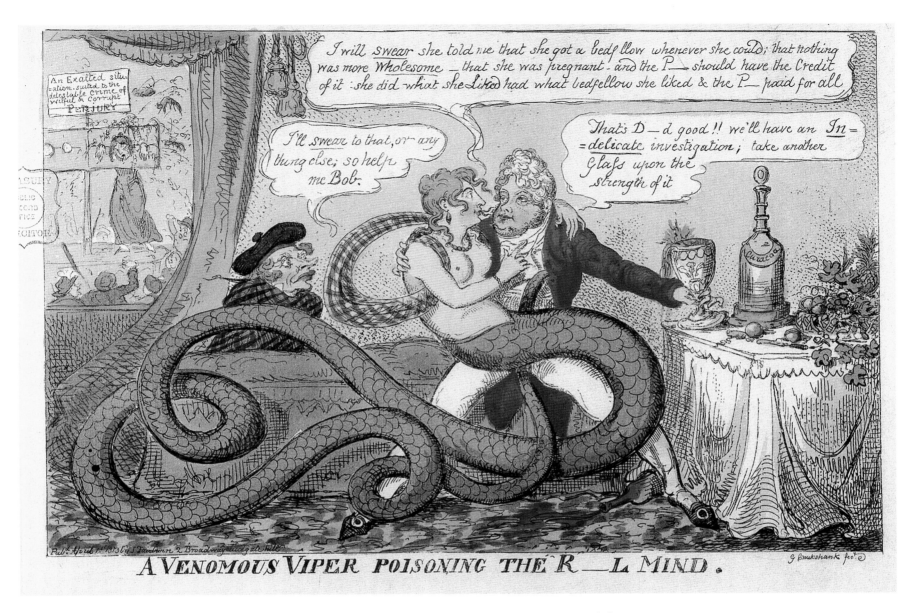

A VENOMOUS VIPER POISONING THE R—L MIND.

**A Venomous Viper Poisoning the R—l Mind**

1 April 1813

GEORGE CRUIKSHANK

*In March 1813 the House of Commons re-examined the Delicate Investigation of 1806, which had inquired into Caroline's alleged adultery in 1801 and 1802. The main accusers were the Douglases, who Caroline believed were 'suborned perjurers'. Lady Douglas became a hate figure. Here she is depicted as a viper telling George that she would, if necessary, take the oath again to allege that Caroline had lovers and had been pregnant. But it was raking over old coals – no one was really interested in the events of twelve years earlier.*

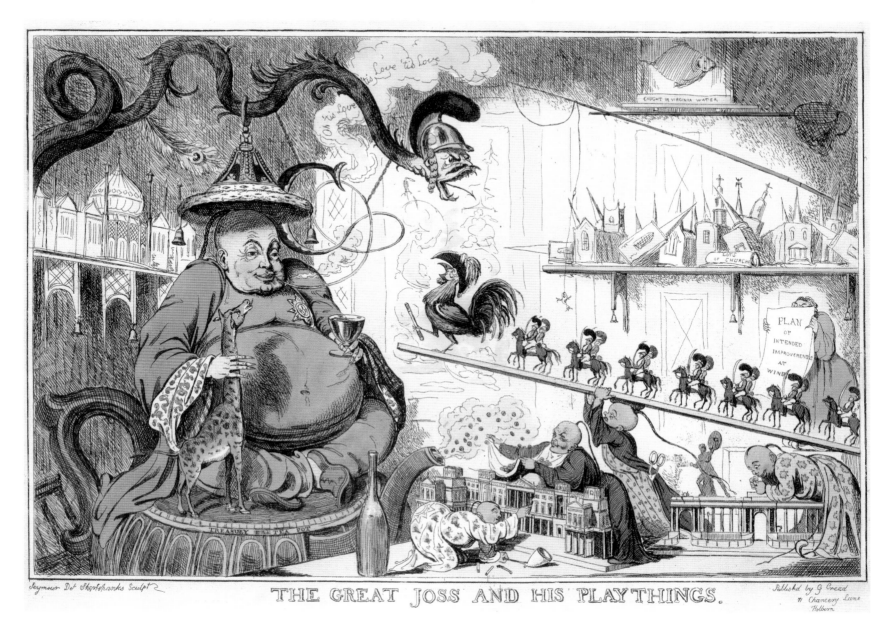

THE GREAT JOSS AND HIS PLAYTHINGS.

**The Great Joss and his Playthings**

February 1829

ROBERT SEYMOUR

*George, as a fat Chinese mandarin, sits cross-legged on the Treasury teapot, which is spouting sovereigns to pay for all his hobbies: architectural projects including the Brighton Pavilion, the remodelled Buckingham Palace, the Decimus Burton arches at Hyde Park Corner, the Achilles statue, some ninety-eight churches; and the fish in the case is a reminder of the works at Virginia Water to provide him with some fishing. His favourite regiment the Life Guards, led by Wellington; the giraffe he kept in his menagrie; the gold cup and the wine bottle complete this striking image of a man who has got away with doing just what he wanted.*

THE CAMELOPARD, or a NEW HOBBY

## The Camelopard, or, A New Hobby

August 1827

WILLIAM HEATH

*The Pasha of Egypt presented a giraffe (with two Nubian attendants) to George, who added it to his menagerie. It was such an amazing animal that it attracted a great deal of attention, becoming a favourite with the caricaturists. Here George and his mistress Lady Conyngham are riding it together – a combined weight that would have certainly broken its back.*

The actual state occasions – the procession down the Royal Mile; the great ball in the Assembly Rooms; the review of troops at Portobello Sands; the service in St Giles; and the banquet on Parliament Hill – were all accompanied by cheering crowds. He was popular: a rather rare experience for George.

The arrangements for the twenty-day visit were left to Walter Scott, who turned it into a tartan extravaganza. Everyone was expected to wear a kilt, including the King. Scott created a series of pageants – it was dubbed the celtification of Scotland – but George himself helped to define what makes Scotland so different. George loved every minute. Appearing in full Highland dress, he was delighted to hear the Scottish toast – 'The Chief of the Clans, the King.' He was prepared to appear every inch a king and from a bill submitted by George Hunter of Token House Yard in Edinburgh it was clear that he was not prepared to stint himself:

> a pair of fine gold shoe rosettes, studded all over with variegated gems…a goatskin Highland purse with a massive gold spring top…three black Morocco belts, a fine gold head ornament for his bonnet consisting of the Royal Scots crown in miniature, set with diamonds, pearls, rubies and emeralds; a large gold brooch pin with variegated Scotch gems; a powder horn finely mounted in fine gold; a fine basket; a Highland sword of polished steel; a pair of fine polished steel Highland pistols; 61 yards of royal satin plaid; 31 yards of royal plaid velvet.

George was also pleased that in Scotland the press praised him. The *Observer* dubbed him 'George the Patriotic'. He had won 'the affection of an unattached and ordinary people, a great and generous people', and all this in his great northern capital, 'not in the smoke of London where he has ever been insulted and reviled.'

George impressed and amassed – he was fond of showing off. His passion for collecting included animals, and he kept a large menagerie of exotic beasts, including a zebra, a leopard, a llama, kangaroos, gnus, monkeys, an ostrich and many other exotic birds. He commissioned oil paintings of many of them, including the giraffe sent to him in 1827, near the end of his reign, by the Pasha of Egypt. This spectacular gift captured the public's imagination and the attention of the satirists.

## Le Mort

11 August 1829

H. B. [JOHN DOYLE]

*After two years the poor giraffe died – an event greeted by the effusive tears of Lady Conyngham and the King. The excessive expression of grief is accompanied by the reactionary Tory Lord Eldon, who had recently made many visits to George to stiffen his opposition to Catholic emancipation. But Anglican supremacy, like the giraffe, was dead. The giraffe was stuffed, and its skeleton preserved, for display at Windsor.*

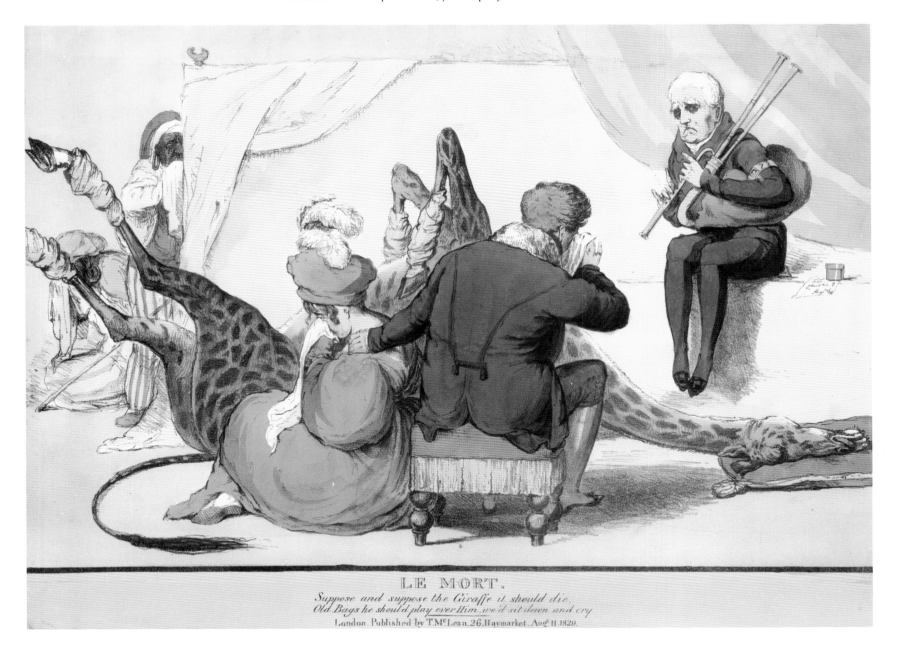

LE MORT.

*Suppose and suppose the Giraffe it should die,*
*Old Bags he should play over Him, we'd sit down and cry.*

London. Published by T. McLean, 26, Haymarket. Aug.t 11 1829.

## The Royal Pavilion, Brighton.
## The Music Room, 1823

JOHN AGAR, AFTER AUGUSTUS PUGIN
AND JAMES STEPHANOFF

*John Nash, commissioned by George to redesign the Pavilion, created an architectural extravaganza – Indian on the outside, Chinese within and bits of Gothic here and there. This room was created to the design of Nash, Frederick Crace and Robert Jones in 1818–20. It was the high point of George's infatuation with chinoiserie. The walls were lacquered in red and gold Chinese landscapes; serpents twisted round pillars; a dragon chimney-piece; Chinese pagodas; a ceiling of small fish-scales; and nine painted glass water-lily chandeliers all supplied with gas, the use of which George had pioneered. One of George's great passions was music. This scene celebrates the concert held on 20 December 1823, conducted by the great Italian composer Gioacchino Rossini. George sits on the left flanked by Lady Conyngham and her daughter.*

# 12 The Builder of Genius

ON COMING OF AGE IN 1783, George received as a gift from his father a Palladian villa designed by William Kent, in Pall Mall, close to what is now Trafalgar Square. George appointed Henry Holland as his architect, who was given the job of converting this small house into a palace suitable for the Prince of Wales.

Holland's initial estimate for the works, submitted that year, was £30,000 (about £3 million in today's money) but over the following twenty years well over ten times that amount was spent, on both the exterior and the lavish interior. Many rooms and galleries were added, the outside of the building faced with Portland stone, a portico of Corinthian columns created (some of which were later re-used in the façade of the National Gallery), and in an act of genius Holland placed a screen of Ionic columns across the courtyard at the front of the house.

George appointed Daguerre, a French interior decorator, to ensure that the furniture, damask hangings, upholstery, looking glasses, carpets, chandeliers and lanterns were not only entirely sumptuous but also in the fashionable Anglo-French style. Within a few years visitors were able to pass from a Chinese Room to the Red Satin Drawing Room, to the Blue Velvet Room, on to the Music Room and the Red Crimson Dining Room where in June 1785 George gave a dinner for four hundred and fifty guests drawn from the great Whig families. Nothing like this had been built before in England – in its grandiose scale, extravagant furnishings and sparkling brilliance. Horace Walpole was won over: for him Carlton House was the 'most perfect palace in Europe'.

All this was possible only through the enthusiastic, creative and whimsical patronage of George. He loved the glitter of glass, the sensuous silks and velvets, the marble from Italy, the gilded furniture from France, and the paintings from Holland. It was a grand stage setting for George to make his appearance – not only as heir apparent but also as the greatest connoisseur of his day.

George IV created Brighton as a major resort town: the population rose from 3,620 in 1786 to 40,000 in 1830. In 1820 the *Sussex Weekly Advertiser* proudly declared, 'The King is to this town what the sun is to our hemisphere.' As Prince, Regent and King, George usually spent between two and four months in Brighton, and the presence of his court created a huge number of jobs for local people: butchers, perfumiers, apothecaries, bakers, grocers, wine merchants, tailors, saddlers, coachmakers, furriers, builders and bootmakers: in 1821 the quarterly account for linen washed was £85.17.1¾d – two years' salary for a housemaid.

George enjoyed going to Brighton because he was popular there: at Christmas three thousand dinners were distributed to the needy poor; the local residents loved the spectacular firework displays that celebrated his arrival; and when George was in town he brought with him soldiers from the First Regiment of Life Guards and the bandsmen from his own band who were very popular with the local tradesmen and innkeepers. George also enjoyed being at what William Wilberforce called 'Piccadilly-by-the-seaside'. In 1815 he told his mother that 'the air and constant riding exercise which I take daily, either on the open road or in the Riding House, agree with me more this year than they almost have ever done.'

In the mid-1780s George rented a small farmhouse for himself and Maria Fitzherbert, close to the sea in the centre of Brighton. Henry Holland, the architect of Carlton House, was commissioned in 1787 to convert this into a charming marine pavilion. Within a few years George had an exquisite, coolly elegant neoclassical villa. George was indifferent to the costs, to the criticisms of MPs, and to the refusal of ministers to meet his debts: he believed that the nation had a duty to fund his lifestyle.

In 1803 George fell out with Holland over a trivial matter and for the next ten years employed various less imaginative architects. The Pavilion was enlarged during a period from 1802 to 1804, and then decorated in the high Chinese style by the Craces. In 1813 he established a partnership with another great figure, John Nash, who was asked to redesign Carlton House yet again, to create new apartments, a grander assembly room, and space to house George's ever-growing collection of paintings.

A MORNING RIDE.

Defigned by I.L.R. — Etch'd by J. Gillray —                                           London, Publish'd Feb.ª 25.ᵗʰ 1804. by H. Humphrey. 27 S.ᵗ James's Street. —

"Yet aft a ragged Cowte's been known
   "To mak a noble Aiver;
"So, Ye may doucely fill a Throne.
   "For a'their clish-ma-claver;

"There, Him at Agincourt wha shone.
   "Few better were or braver;
"An'yet, wi'funny, queer Sir John
   "He was an unco shaver
      "For monie a day." Burns.

a A Colt.   b A Horse.   c Talk or Patter.

**A Morning Ride**

25 February 1804

JAMES GILLRAY

*The Prince of Wales is seen riding with his Secretary John McMahon, in front of the great façade of Carlton House. Having passed through the gates, visitors crossed an open courtyard to enter the house through a neoclassical Greek portico. George changed the interior of the house many times but the great impressive façade remained until it was demolished in 1827, near the end of his reign. The verse at the bottom refers to the fact that at this time George III was ill – the Prince was being flatteringly compared to Prince Hal during the illness of Henry IV.*

137

## THE JOSS AND HIS FOLLY
### *An Extract of an overland Dispatch.*

I stare at it from out my casement,
And ask for what is such a place meant. *Byron*

——The queerest of all the queer sights
    I've set sight on; –
Is, the *what d'ye cal'-t thing*, here,
    THE FOLLY at Brighton
The outside – huge teapots,
    all drill'd round with holes,
Relieved by extinguishers,
    sticking on poles:
The inside – all tea-things,
    and dragons, and bells,
The show rooms – *all* show,
    the sleeping rooms – cells.

But the grand Curiosity
    's not to be seen –
The owner himself –
    an old fat MANDARIN;
A patron of painters
    who copy designs,
That grocers and tea-dealers
    hang up for signs:
Hence teaboard-taste artists
    gain rewards and distinction,
Hence the title of 'TEAPOT'
    shall last to extinction.

**The Joss and his Folly**

July 1820

GEORGE CRUIKSHANK

---

However, the traditional architects struck back, and Peter Pindar composed an epigram that would have appealed to Soane:

> Master Nash, Master Nash
> You merit the lash,
> For debauching the taste of our Heir to the throne:
> Then cross not the seas
> To rob the Chinese,
> But learn to be wise from VITRUVIUS and SOANE.

George had indeed become fascinated by and infatuated with the arts of the East – having sent his own courier to rifle the great treasure houses there and to bring back what he could. Nash was asked to redesign the Pavilion, which resulted in a building that was Indian on the outside and Chinese on the inside.

The resultant building was a magnificent and idiosyncratic mishmash of styles, including Gothic, with minarets and bulbous, onion-shaped domes. It was an audacious triumph: Brighton Pavilion is still one of the most remarkable buildings in Europe. Hazlitt called it a collection of 'stone pumpkins and pepper boxes…anything more fantastical was never seen.' Sydney Smith made his celebrated comment that it was as if 'St Paul's had come down to the seaside and pupped.'

Inside the Pavilion George set out to astonish, and he succeeded. The Music Room was his most stunning creation. The walls were panelled with Chinese scenes in gold and red lacquer, serpents twined around curtains and columns, all under a vast dome decorated with diminishing fish-scales holding up nine huge chandeliers in the shape of Chinese water lilies. The Banqueting Room was fit for an Eastern emperor – the central chandelier hung from the ceiling surrounded by large palm leaves, a silver dragon and lotus flowers; the walls were rich with scenes in red, gold and blue; and on the table there was a dinner service that had been made so delicately by Sèvres that it was delivered to the French King, Louis XVI, piece by piece. The overall effect was dazzling – nothing like it had been seen before.

In these rooms George never lost sight of his two priorities – dining and music. The cost of the Music Room was £45,000 (about £5 million in today's money). The Banqueting Room cost £42,000 and, its huge chandelier, weighing over a ton, cost a further £11,000 (about £1 million in today's money).

George was always very keen to use the latest technological advances in construction – he took the risk of using cast iron in the Gothic conservatory at Carlton House and having seen its

## Imperial Botany, or, A Peep at Josephine's Collection of English Exoticks

1814

HOLMES

This engaging satire shows the Empress Josephine in her house outside Paris, Malmaison, where she lived virtually in exile after Napoleon abandoned her, and where she created a magnificent garden. Among her exotic plants are a Wellington laurel and an Eldon burr. Pride of place goes to a Royal Sunflower, but twining around its stem is another plant, Love in Idleness. Josephine says of her sunflower, 'Ah you rogue! Why that is a favourite plant of English ladies – I must cut away that Love in Idleness or it will ruin my plant.' Napoleon has bloomed but his flower is about to drop. This may well have reflected Josephine's feelings, but they were not put to the test: a few months after this satire was published she died from a throat infection.

**An Imperial Vomit**

4 June 1815

WILLIAMS

*George is given the major role in getting Napoleon to cough up all his territorial conquests, which are falling into a bucket labelled George Prince and Co. George condescendingly addresses Napoleon as 'my little fellow'.*

**Boney's Meditations on the Island of St Helena, or, The Devil Addressing the Sun**

August 1815

GEORGE CRUIKSHANK

*When the* Bellerophon *anchored off Torbay on 26 July 1815 Napoleon wrote to George asking for the hospitality of England to be extended to him. But in no way was the Cabinet going to revoke the decision to exile Napoleon to the remote, inaccessible and inhospitable island of St Helena. Napoleon is shown straddling the rocky entrance to St Helena quoting, to a resplendent sun of the Regent, words from Milton's* Paradise Lost*: 'How I hate thy beams, that bring to my remembrance from what state I fell.' George did not do this all by himself – the rays from the sun contain the names of the main allied commanders.*

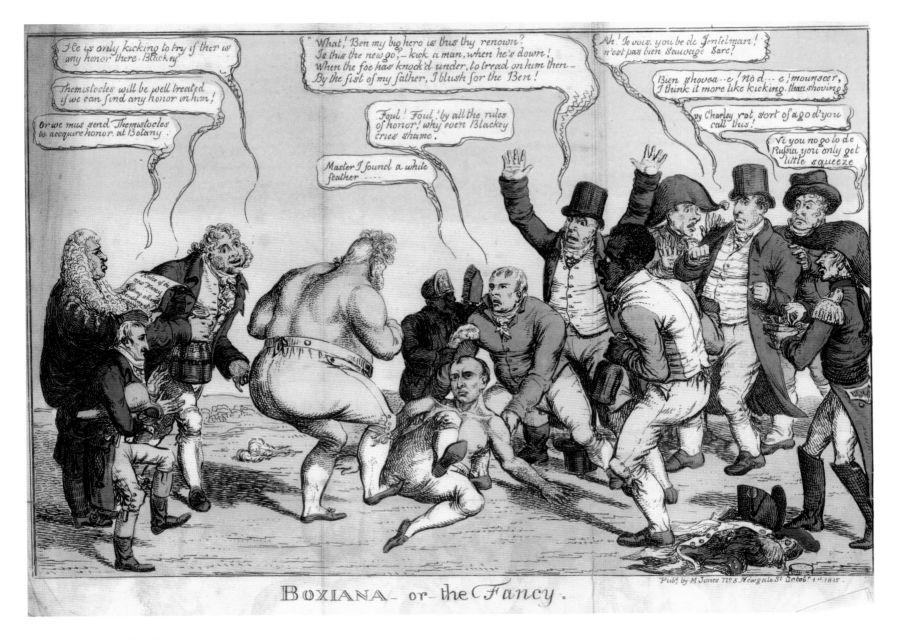

**Boxiana, or, The Fancy**

1 October 1815

WILLIAMS

*This print reproaches George for rejecting Napoleon's plea for refuge in England and so he kicks him while he is down. George enjoyed going to the bare-knuckle boxing fights on the Downs outside Brighton. At one of the fights a boxer was killed and George gave an annuity to his widow.*

*During his coronation twelve boxers were employed to control the crowds.*

*Four lines of Tom Moore's poem are quoted by a bystander:*

*What! Ben my big hero is this thy renoun?*
*Is this the new go? – Kick a man when he's down!*
*When the foe has knocked under to tread on him then –*
*By the fist of my father I blush for thee Ben!*

# 14 Unloved and Unwanted

AFTER 1815 Britain came close to revolution. The years following the defeat of Napoleon saw economic distress and political turmoil as tens of thousands of soldiers and sailors joined the ranks of the workless. Luddites wrecked the new machines that replaced hand labour and at Pentrich in Nottinghamshire in 1817 rioters were hanged. In August 1819 the Manchester Yeomanry rode into a large crowd that had gathered at St Peter's Fields to hear the radical orator Henry Hunt: eleven were killed and four hundred wounded. This outrage was instantly labelled the Peterloo Massacre. Habeas corpus was suspended and the embryonic trades unions were banned. Sidmouth, the Home Secretary, used an extensive network of spies – one of whom, Edwards, betrayed a group of conspirators in Cato Street, who had been planning to assassinate the entire Cabinet in 1820.

The whole Establishment was under threat. In December 1819 the government reacted by bringing in the repressive Six Acts, which prohibited meetings of over fifty people; imposed heavy penalties for seditious libel; and increased Stamp Duty on newspapers and cheap pamphlets by four pence – thus putting 'twopenny trash' beyond the pockets of the poor. In Italy Shelley dreamt that anarchy would sweep across England:

> Last came Anarchy: he rode
> On a white horse, splashed with blood;
> He was pale even to the lips,
> Like Death in the Apocalypse,
>
> And he wore a kingly crown;
> And in his grasp a sceptre shone;
> On his brow this mark I saw –
> 'I AM GOD, AND KING, AND LAW!'
>
> With a pace stately and fast,
> Over English land he passed,
> Trampling to a mire of blood
> The adoring multitude.

George III, living as a recluse at Windsor, had not been seen for ten years and the Regent, as head of state, was held in contempt. Already he appeared as a hangover from another age but his way of life was, for the first time, seen as undermining the very constitution.

It was George's great misfortune to suffer at the hands of some of the most brilliant caricaturists England has ever produced. But this misfortune was heightened by a change in printing technology. The prints of James Gillray and Isaac Cruikshank were produced from copperplates with the images printed and sold individually: it was not possible to print extended text alongside them. But this method of etching was about to be challenged by engraving on blocks of boxwood. The woodblock could be mounted alongside typeset text and the two printed together. This led to the decline of separate caricature prints. Political cartoons and journalism were married and the illustrated political pamphlet was born. These were printed not in scores or in hundreds, but in thousands and tens of thousands, and sold for a few coppers. The devastating satires attacking George were no longer just amusements for the political and informed coteries of London; they were now available in drawing rooms, parlours and workshops across the country.

The most famous pamphlet, first published in 1819, was *The Political House that Jack Built*. The satirical verses were written by the radical publisher William Hone, who had been unsuccessfully prosecuted for libel in 1817, and the accompanying wood engravings were provided by Isaac Cruikshank's son George. Their pamphlet attacked the repressive measures of the Government and defended the freedom of the press. It struck at the very top of society: the most devastating of the drawings was 'The Dandy of Sixty' (George) 'who plundered the wealth that lay in the house that Jack built.' Within six months forty editions were published and it was little wonder that *The Political House that Jack Built* was dubbed 'Gunpowder in Boxwood'. The Regent attended a meeting of the Privy Council and 'laid it on the table without saying a word'. He wanted Hone to be prosecuted but the Lord Chancellor persuaded him not to press for this 'for fear of the consequences'.

A brief media war broke out, with Tory and City interests financing a pamphlet entitled *A Parody on the Political House that Jack Built, or, The Real House that Jack Built*, by

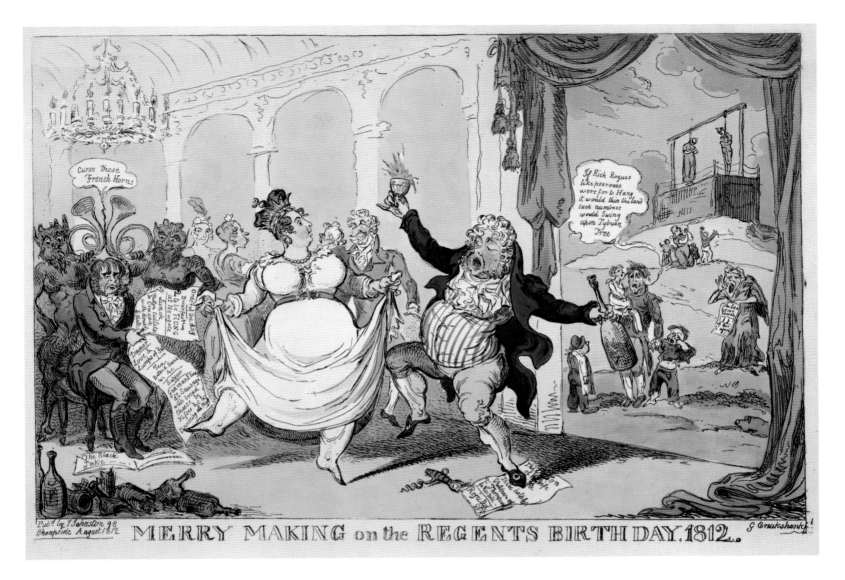

**MERRY MAKING on the REGENTS BIRTH DAY, 1812**

M. Adams. The woodcut depicted George in a noble pose, admired by Britannia, and with the epigraph, 'Great talents deserve great offices.' It ran to only one edition.

The return of Caroline, the divorce proceedings, the Bill of Pains and Penalties, were all seized upon by Hone. He picked up on the plaintive excuse used by Italian witnesses against Caroline when they were under the withering cross-examination of Brougham: *Non mi ricordo!* Hone quickly created a pamphlet bearing that title, and another, *The Queen's Matrimonial Ladder*, depicting George as cat's meat.

## Merry Making on the Regent's Birthday, 1812

August 1812

GEORGE CRUIKSHANK

*This print makes a rare social comparison, between royalty and the state of the ragged poor – whose petition to aid helpless children is stamped on by George. The pauper in front of the gallows says, 'If rich rogues like poor ones were for to hang it would thin the land such numbers would swing upon Tyburn Tree.' A carefree George frolics with Isabella Hertford. The first item on his Order of the Day is 'Breakfast – 2 to be hung at Newgate.' This print was in George's private collection, which was sold to the Library of Congress in Washington in 1921.*

## Royal Embarkation, or, Bearing Britannia's Hope from a Bathing Machine to the Royal Barge

18 August 1819

GEORGE CRUIKSHANK

*On 16 August, charging into a crowd of over 80,000 people calling for radical reform, the cavalry killed eleven and wounded four hundred – the Peterloo Massacre. George sent a message of support to the Manchester magistrates who had ordered the charge. Here, two days later, with Britain seething with unrest, George is shown leaving the delights of the naked bathing belles of Brighton and returning to his yacht to go on to the Regatta at Cowes.*

## A Mysterious Box on the Head of Royalty

14 October 1819

*An interesting print not recorded in the British Museum. The radicals had taken up the running and some even predicted the overthrow of the monarchy. Here the words of Ezekiel, Chapter 21, Verses 25–27, fall upon George's head:*

*25. And thou profane, wicked Prince of Israel, whose day is come when iniquity will have an end.*
*26. Thus saith the Lord God: Remove the diadem and take off the crown: this shall not be the same: exalt him that is low and abase him that is high.*
*27. I will overturn, overturn, overturn it: and it shall be no more until he come whose right it is, and I will give it him!*

This is THE MAN – all shaven and shorn,
All cover'd with Orders – and all folorn;
THE DANDY OF SIXTY,
     who bows with a grace,
And has *taste* in wigs, collars
     cuirasses, and lace;
Who, to tricksters and fools
     leaves the State and its treasure,
And, when Britain's in tears,
     sails about at his pleasure,
Who spurn'd from his presence
     the Friends of his youth,
And now has not one
     who will tell him the truth;
Who took to his counsels,
     in evil hour,
The Friends to the Reasons
     of lawless Power;
That back the Public Informer
     who
Would put down the *Thing*,
     that, in spite of new Acts,
And attempts to restrain it,
     by Soldiers or Tax
Will *poison* the Vermin,
That plunder the Wealth,
That lay in the House,
That Jack built.

Great offices will have great talents

## The Dandy of Sixty

1819

GEORGE CRUIKSHANK

*This woodcut appeared in* The Political House that Jack Built.
*It was so popular that it was issued as a separate print with
verses by William Hone. Robert Cruikshank, George's brother,
cashed in by threatening to issue a similar print and so on
23 May 1820 Carlton House paid him £70 for the copyright
of a caricature titled* The Dandy of Sixty.

## A Parody on the Political House that Jack Built, or, The Real House that Jack Built

1820

*This was paid for by City merchants and bankers as a
riposte to Hone's pamphlet.*

Great talents deserve great offices

This is the MAN
     whose birthright's his own;
Who boasts not his orders,
     but treats them as HONE;
The MONARCH OF SIXTY,
     who sprang from a race,
The pride of the world,
     the boast of our days;
That when Britain's in tears
     he relief has refused
who by Tricksters and Fools
     has been falsely accused
That when Britain's in tears
     he relief has refused;
They who spurn from their presence
     the friends of their youth,

And now will not hear one
     who tells them the truth;
Who have threat'ned the Men,
     Who oppose lawless power,
Who are slandered and scofft at
     by the PUBLIC
     INSTRUCTOR,
Who, with two-penny trash,
     has abus'd that good Thing,
That has called for new Acts
     that Truth may restrain it,
Nor Soldiers nor Tax;
For t'would harbour the Vermin,
That injure the Wealth,
That lays in the House
That Jack built.

## The Cradle Hymn

July 1820

ISAAC CRUIKSHANK

*George, as a baby, though holding a corkscrew, is surrounded by toys and is rocked by Sidmouth in a cradle surmounted by a Chinese pagoda. Castlereagh dries a napkin at the fire and Canning takes away a smelling chamberpot. In the broadside that accompanies the print Sidmouth tries to reassure the King:*

*The Queen's return's a trifling matter,*
*Let her face us if she dare;*
*We will shake our Green Bag at her,*
*She will ne'er be crowned I swear.*

*The 'green bags' held barristers' briefs – used in the divorce trial. This was just the complacent reassurance that George fatefully accepted.*

**Advice from the Other World, or,**
**A Peep in the Magic Lanthorn**

August 1820

GEORGE CRUIKSHANK

*In the wake of Peterloo, Pitt's ghost returns to show George what could happen to his Government – the edifice of the nation is burning while his leading ministers are hanged. George promises to mend his ways under the threat of political retribution.*

ROYAL GAMBOLS!! or the OLD OAK IN DANGER.

*Published September 1820, by John Fairburn, Broadway, Ludgate Hill.*

**Royal Gambols, or, The Old Oak in Danger**

September 1820

LEWIS MARKS

*George swings merrily between Lady Conyngham and Lady Hertford while radical devils hack at the oak of England and ministers try to support it. Wellington is having his arm cut off while the army sleeps silently. George's capricious and indulgent behaviour threatens the monarchy itself.*

## Head and Brains!

November 1820

V[OWL]ES

*On 10 November the Bill of Pains and Penalties, an attempt to dissolve the royal marriage and strip Caroline of her titles, was withdrawn. The balloon of persecution and malice is burst. A cherub, with the blast of public opinion, blows away the crown, which is divided between the King and his wife – George is melancholy, Caroline's image is flattering. His half of the crown is dimmed, hers is solid. His ribbon is in tatters. In Covent Garden on the day the Bill was dropped the audience interrupted the performance with cries of 'God Save the Queen' and eventually the company, to a cheering audience, sang God Save the King, but replaced the last word with 'Queen'.*

**Fishing for Popularity, or, Catching Gudgeons, at Brighton!**

January 1821

To re-establish his popularity after the coronation George goes to Brighton fishing for compliments from the locals but they seem intent on celebrating by drinking as much as they can. All the cartoons published by John Fairburn were hostile to George and they always presented him in the worst light. He was in fact very popular in Brighton.

# 15 The Divorce

ON THE DEATH OF HIS FATHER on 29 January 1820 George fell seriously ill with a chest infection that turned into pleurisy. Some believed that Britain was about to experience the shortest reign after the longest. The gravity of this illness did not stop George calling for a copy of the Anglican prayer book and, in an act of petulance, striking Caroline's name from the liturgy. A wiser man would have done nothing as Caroline was almost at the point of not returning to England. But as she was now Queen, she was so deeply offended that she packed up her furniture and plate in Pesaro and set off for England.

By April the Prime Minister, Liverpool, was so alarmed at the prospect of her returning that he agreed to offer Caroline £50,000 (£5 million in today's money) to stay abroad. A year earlier Henry Brougham had suggested only £35,000, which made him doubly surprised to be asked to negotiate on the Government's behalf and prevent her returning to England. It was an extraordinary appointment because Brougham, known to his Whig friends as 'Old Wickedshifts', had his own agenda: to use the return of Caroline to so embarrass the Government that it could be turned out of office. He travelled to France to meet Caroline and only mentioned the higher payment as she was about to embark. At the same time a Radical MP, Alderman Wood, had established contact with Caroline and was encouraging her to return.

Caroline's return was like a royal progress. The royal yacht did not turn up at Calais and so she took an ordinary packet ferry, the *Prince Leopold*, on 4 June. Nearing Dover she received a royal salute from the guns at Dover Castle and as the packet could not dock she risked a small boat – a brilliant touch that pleased the crowds lining the harbour. She was dressed modestly in a black dress and a black satin hat with feathers: she looked like a queen. A band greeted her; banners were waved proclaiming 'God Save Queen Caroline.' Her horses were removed from the traces, and the people of Dover dragged her coach through the town. It was like an election rally and Caroline obliged by waving from the hotel balcony.

In Canterbury the corporation greeted her with loyal addresses. In Sittingbourne the bells of all the churches were rung and a group of churchmen, who could not officially pray for her, turned out to cheer her. As she approached London she was met by the Radical MPs Sir Francis Burdett and Sir Robert Wilson, and she was taken to Alderman Wood's house in South Audley Street, which was besieged by a great crowd for several days. Caroline was the darling of the people. At night gangs roamed the streets of London insisting that householders put candles in their windows to show their support for the Queen. They knocked out the windows in the houses of Government ministers such as Sidmouth, and even the windows of Wellington's carriage were shattered.

The King told his secretaries to trawl all the Government offices for any information about Caroline. The material was bundled up, together with the findings of the Milan Commission, the Delicate Investigation of 1806 and the further inquiry of 1813, and put into two green barristers' brief bags – one for the House of Lords and one for the House of Commons. On 6 June, as Liverpool informed the House of Lords that the King had sent them certain papers, the green bags lay upon the table in the centre of the Chamber. Green bags had been used before, but on this occasion they were seized upon by the cartoonists and became symbolic of the whole issue. If there was a green bag for Caroline's adulteries, there must surely be an even bigger green bag for George's.

The Lords decided to set up a secret committee to examine and assess the evidence. They were under constant pressure from the King, who demanded that his ministers should expose Caroline's behaviour. George even toyed with the idea of getting rid of Liverpool and put out feelers to Tierney and Grey suggesting that if they were to form a Whig government he would be prepared to concede Catholic emancipation – so much for his principled stand for the Church of England. Caroline was also under pressure from the Radicals not to accept any settlement with the King but to put her case to the people. The negotiations between Wellington and Brougham from 14 to 19 June came to grief over the liturgy.

The Queen's cause was taken up not only by Radical MPs but also by forces outside Parliament such as Francis Place the tailor, William Hone the publisher of satirical pamphlets, and John Gast, a Radical shipwright. Gast summoned a meeting of artisans in a pub in the East End of London to condemn spying in all its forms and to present a petition to Caroline that within a

**Paving the Way for a Royal Divorce**

1 October 1816

WILLIAMS

This print, which appeared in the Scourge, is the earliest to show George's enthusiasm for the divorce. Gleefully he picks on the evidence from his spies and urges his reluctant ministers to react – they didn't.

**Reflection. To be, or Not to Be?**

11 February 1820

ISAAC CRUIKSHANK

*With George III dead the new King fears the worst. On 10 February the Cabinet refused his demands for an immediate divorce. George insisted that Caroline's name be omitted from the liturgy but at the proclamation the cry was, 'God save the Queen!' This prescient print foretold the disasters that were about to overwhelm the King despite being published within only a fortnight of his accession.*

fortnight had nearly thirty thousand signatures. Pamphlets parodied the new King as Henry VIII or Nero; broadsides were posted up in the streets of London; and scores of prints depicted him as a lecherous buffoon.

No event in history has been more savagely caricatured nor the main players so distorted as in these prints, which were clearly libellous but had become propaganda for each side. The American ambassador to the Court of St James's was amazed at 'the boundless rage of the Press'. For six months the country was consumed with a fever and the only things that anyone was interested in were the trial and the divorce.

There were meetings and addresses of support from all the major towns; extra troops had to be posted in London, particularly after one regiment laid down its arms; and Wellington arranged for small troops of armed, mounted soldiers to patrol the main streets. When some Crown witnesses were spotted arriving at Dover they were abused and physically attacked. Civil unrest was in the air and the summer months of 1820 witnessed the real possibility of a popular uprising against the government of the day. Nothing like this had been seen since the Gordon Riots of 1780 and it was to pave the way for the popular demonstrations of 1830 in favour of parliamentary reform and the Chartist movement in the 1840s.

In early July the secret committee found that proceedings should be started against the Queen. Lord Eldon, the Lord Chancellor, had unearthed an extraordinary precedent, namely a Bill of Pains and Penalties, which had last been used after the Jacobite Rebellion in 1745. If passed, this Bill would dissolve the marriage of Caroline and George and deprive her of all her titles – in effect removing her from the kingdom. It had to be passed by both Houses of Parliament. As it was a Private Bill, witnesses could be summoned to appear before either House, which meant that it was in effect a trial. It was a constitutional device designed to convict the Queen of treason and to avoid recourse to the normal courts of the land by calling into play the high court of Parliament. It was a travesty of justice and a constitutional monstrosity.

The second reading was scheduled for 17 August, just six weeks later – that was all the time allowed for the defence to get its act together. It was an outrage, since if the Bill became enacted the King would get a divorce without any of his own actions being taken into account – it would be one-way adultery. Everyone, including Brougham, held back from threatening to reveal the King's own infidelities and his marriage to Mrs

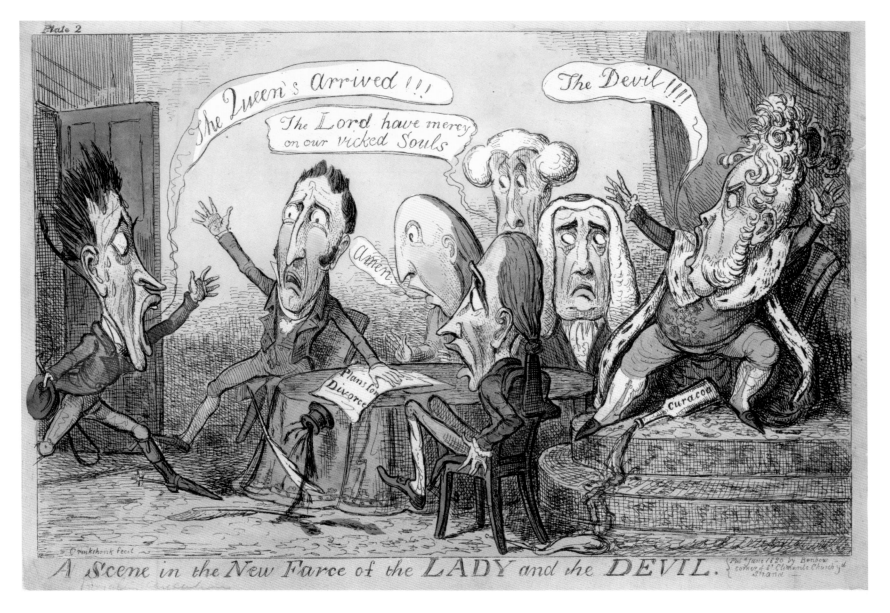

**A Scene in the New Farce of the Lady and the Devil**

June 1820

ISAAC CRUIKSHANK

The Government through Lord Brougham offered an annuity of £50,000 to Caroline to stay in France and renounce her position as Queen. She immediately set out for England, landing on 4 June and entering London in state on 6 June. This is what George and his ministers had long dreaded. The archbishop says 'Lord have mercy on our souls' to which the Prime Minister, Liverpool, adds 'Amen,' while Castlereagh and Sidmouth, startled and appalled, spill the ink for their divorce plans. From now on they were not in charge of events.

Fitzherbert. However, Gillray's famous print published in 1786, *The Morning After Marriage*, was republished on the day of the second reading.

Caroline knew how to appeal to the masses – vulgarity attracted vulgarity. In August she sent a letter to *The Times*, drafted by William Cobbett, which criticized the King: 'You have pursued me with hatred and scorn....You sent me sorrowing through the world, and even in my sorrows pursued me with unrelenting persecution.' Caroline could not have matched such eloquence in her own clumsy prose, but what Cobbett wrote was the truth.

The Government presented its case and the first witness was called on 21 August – Teodoro Majocchi. He testified to seeing Caroline and Bergami sleeping together in a tent on the deck of the *polucca*. He was destroyed by Brougham's cross-examination on the following day when Majocchi had to stutter in Italian, '*Non mi ricordo*' – 'I do not remember.' Another witness, Louise Demont, Caroline's chambermaid, whose evidence was crucial to the Crown's case, had to resort to the French version, '*Je ne me rappelle pas.*'

The court adjourned on 9 September to allow Brougham to prepare the defence. He opened on 3 October with a brilliant display of forensic skill that lasted two days. His witnesses, who were mainly the English members of the Queen's suite, impressed their Lordships. Brougham made great play of the

## Grand Entrance to Bamboozl'Em

February 1821

THEODORE LANE

*Theodore Lane was a young actor who supplemented his meagre earnings through working as a caricaturist. He was to die very young when he fell to his death through a plate-glass window. He produced in 1821 a series of prints that ridiculed Caroline and her lover. This print appeared well after the event of Caroline's entry to London and was part of the campaign to discredit her. The Queen, ungartered and décolleté, wearing a cap of liberty, and Alderman Wood dressed as a jester, ride through the city on asses to be greeted by the Radicals Henry Hunt and Francis Burdett. Caroline's supporters are depicted as dangerous reformers, who cynically seized upon her as a tool to further their cause. The message is clear: support Caroline and you support anarchy and revolution.*

O ENTRANCE TO BAMBOOZL'EM.

Published by G. Humphrey 27 St James's St Feb 1821

| dy Ann Bagpipe principal tch Fiddler her M——y ith an accom- raniment of ll around the ad note how ve Flock. | Her most Graceful M——y Columbine B——i alias Mother Red Cap 2d Queen of all the Radicals, Whigs, Hoaxers & B——i in all her looks and Brandy in her eye. | Countess Patois Bourgois The Elegant Accomplished Sister of Bart——o The Fancy-Man | The Dandy Standard Bear-er alias Young Absolute | Billy By-Blow of Black-heath in charge of the Nursery | Lieut Hummem 1st Champion & Knight of St Columbine | Lieutt Flim Flam 2nd Champion & Knight of the Smelling Bottle | Two Proteges and Bosom Friends of her M——y | A long train of concomitant Blessings to add to the Peace, Comfort, Relief, and Happiness of that first rate Martyr Broad-shoulder--ed and patient Bull. |

"Ah! sure such a pair was never seen so justly form'd to meet by nature"
Dedicated to Old Bags

### 'Ah! Sure Such a Pair was Never Seen so Justly Form'd to Meet by Nature'

23 June 1820

GEORGE CRUIKSHANK

*This was the print that spelt the King's doom. It was the first to feature the famous green bags that George had sent down on the day of the Queen's arrival – one to the House of Lords and one to the House of Commons. They contained the evidence of the Queen's misconduct that had been gathered by the Milan Commission. Government papers were sent in this way as a matter of course but Brougham seized upon it brilliantly by saying 'If the King had a green bag, the Queen might have one too.' This was fatal to George's case – his bag is bigger than hers and the buckled garter around his vast girth tails off like a limp penis. This inspired image dominated the debate for the next six months and the great pear-shaped figures of George and Caroline anticipated the pear-shaped caricatures of Louis-Philippe of France in the 1830s.*

deceitful, underhand way the Government had gone about collecting evidence, including paying witnesses. When he sought to recall one witness who was suspected of suborning another it was found that the man had fled to Italy. The whole process was beginning to look more like a conspiracy than a trial.

Caroline attended most of the sittings of the court – grave and silent, a much-wronged woman. On 6 November the Government's majority was only twenty-eight, but as the divorce clause remained in the Bill the bishops could not support it at the third reading and the majority fell to nine. On 19 November Liverpool had to abandon the Bill. The Queen was acquitted even though many believed she was guilty. Cobbett summed it up rather well: 'Caroline was an injured wife, although I do not doubt she was a depraved woman.'

When the Bill was lost George blamed his ministers – which he was ever ready to do. But the fault was his. He had determined the fatal strategy: he had insisted, against advice, upon demanding a divorce and he had rejected any compromise. His hatred of Caroline, built up over the years, had to burst out. It warped his judgment, with dire consequences.

George was so determined to divorce Caroline that he was incapable of appreciating that the evidence gathered by the Milan Commission was tainted. Stories about Caroline's adultery could be easily bought and all the witnesses had to be paid handsomely to come to London. He failed to foresee that not one of the witnesses would stand up to rigorous cross-examination in an English court. The King, and not the Cabinet, drove events – and he proved to be a disastrous coachman.

The Government might have won if it had discovered a Sicilian cook, Iacinto Greco, who had served Caroline at Syracuse in 1816. Greco told a Foreign Office agent that one night, on opening a door in the saloon, he saw

> …the Princess on the sofa at the farther end of the saloon – Bergami was standing between her legs which were in his arms – his breeches were down and his back towards the door at which I was. I saw the Princess's thighs quite naked – Bergami was moved backwards and forwards and in the very act with the Princess.

Bergami noticed him and the next day Greco was fired. Greco told the English agent that he had not come forward because his wife had told him that if he went to England his head would be cut off.

The victory in November was the high point of Caroline's crusade. The public had had enough of the whole episode and

The Bag unsealed, out flew the Feinds of Hell –
a motley group, with venomed Harpid Tongues prepared to do their
Masters errand & fully bent with dire Satanic Rage to Poison
every source of Virtue, Peace
& Justice
Curse the Stench
Lies
oh the Cursed filth we have wade through
Green Bag
Pandora's box was nothing to this
OPENING the GREEN BAG, or the Feinds of Hell let loose – Disappointing to the hopes of the Parliament
Derogatory from the Dignity of the Crown, & Injurious to the best Intrest of the Empire
London Pub 8 July 1820 by S W Fores 41 Piccadilly

soon everything cooled down – time was on the side of the Government, and George.

George had a very rough time at the hands of the cartoonists in 1820, but in 1821 it was Caroline's turn. Theodore Lane produced a series of amusing cartoons depicting the relationship between Caroline and Bergami in very explicit terms. In a speech on 23 January 1821, George offered to provide an annuity to the Queen and this ended the affair. In March she accepted and in the meantime the House of Commons had resolved the liturgy issue by two votes in the King's favour. Mrs

**Opening the Green Bag, or,**
**The Fiends of Hell Let Loose**

July 1820

*Once the committee had started to examine the contents of the green bag, nothing could stop the venomous accusations surfacing. The Government simply did not know how to contain it. Castlereagh flees to the left; Sidmouth throws up his arms in horror; and on the right Canning, who is alleged to have been one of Caroline's lovers, is thrown to the floor.*

## Public Opinion!

July 1820

WILLIAM HEATH

*George has lost it. John Bull is going to see fair play and not even the combined efforts of Liverpool, Castlereagh, Sidmouth and Eldon can make George popular. Brougham, the Queen's lawyer, claimed that he had saved her, and he did successfully use the trial proceedings to appeal to a much wider court – public opinion.*

## The Kettle Calling the Pot Ugly Names

12 August 1820

JOHN MARSHALL

*This was published just before the trial began. The King is more caricatured than the Queen and he hisses while Caroline, with a smile, remarks 'Remember when the Judgement's weak, the prejudice is strong.'*

Arbuthnot recorded that on 7 February when the King went to Drury Lane the National Anthem was sung three times and the cheering lasted for fifteen minutes – 'immense acclamations, the whole pit standing up, hurrahing and waving their hats.'

There was no longer a cause to fight for and Caroline appeared to be a greedy woman grabbing what she could. On 5 May Napoleon died on St Helena and when an eager courtier told the King the news by saying, 'I have, Sir, to congratulate you: your greatest enemy is dead,' George responded, 'Is she, by God!'

The coronation was announced in June and Caroline decided that she would like to attend. But the Government supported George's view that it was the King alone who decided the details of the coronation and if he decided to exclude Caroline then that was what would happen. When she turned up at Westminster Abbey, accompanied by one of her former lovers, she was turned away, and when she tried to enter through Westminster Hall the doors were slammed in her face. On the following day Walter Scott said that Caroline's cause was 'a fire of straw which has now burnt to the very embers. Those who try to blow it into light again will only blacken their hands and noses.'

Shortly afterwards Caroline succumbed to a strange internal illness, described as 'an obstruction of the bowels attended with inflammation'. In her last few days she was well enough to sign her will, destroy most of her papers, including her own *Red Book*, which was allegedly her description of her relationship with George. On 7 August 1821 she died. George learnt of her death while travelling to Ireland and he left the steamboat at Dublin dead drunk.

The public had been entertained for six months and although the Radicals had tried to exploit the situation politically, there was a general festive mood – it was rather like reading the *News of the World* every day. Caroline had won but her reputation had been blown apart; she was brazen, foul-mouthed, and shameless – she liked to wear skirts that were too short and dresses that were too low for her squat figure. The trial had shown that if it was treason to sleep with the Queen, there had been no shortage of traitors. Max Beerbohm, at the end of the 19th century, described it well: 'Fate wrote her a most tremendous tragedy, and she played it in tights.'

**To Be, or, Not to Be!**

July 1820

LEWIS MARKS

*Caroline had formally asked the Privy Council to be crowned at the approaching coronation. Brougham pleaded her case on 5 July and the Council rejected it on 10 July.*

**King Henry VIII. Act II Scene IV**

August 1820

LEWIS MARKS

This is the first print comparing George to Henry VIII, who also failed to obtain a divorce. Catherine of Aragon's famous speech, 'Sir, I desire you do me right and justice, And to bestow your pity on me,' falls on deaf ears. George is consoled with a decanter of curaçao while Castlereagh stamps on Magna Carta.

**The Bone of Contention, or, Political Merry Thought Being a New Way to Get Married**

28 August 1820

JOHN MARSHALL

*This was the beginning of the trial, when the witnesses' evidence was becoming known. The wishbone of the marriage and of the constitution is being pulled apart and George is already showing his annoyance with his ministers Sidmouth, Castlereagh and Liverpool who are all pulling behind him: 'D[am]n you all why don't you pull you vagabonds.'*

## Outside View of the Crown Tap

10 September 1820

JOHN MARSHALL

*George, sitting on a privy, pulls out of the green bag a great dollop of filth. The caption says, 'He put in his thumb, and pull'd out a plum/Saying what a great fool am I.' A bulbous-nosed John Bull contemptuously tells the king that if he does not stop it he will get shat on.*

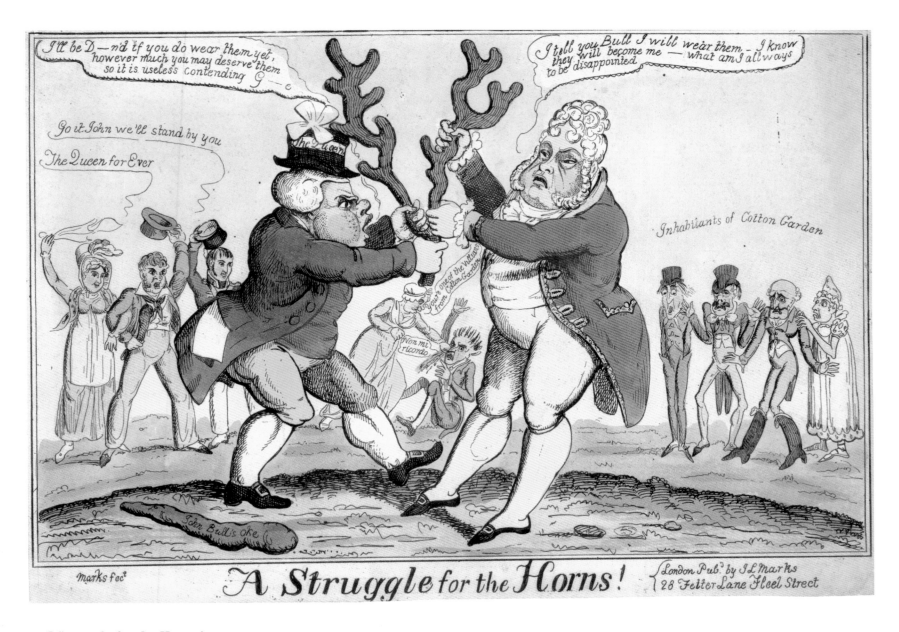

## A Struggle for the Horns!

September 1820

LEWIS MARKS

George wants to wear a cuckold's horns to confirm his wife's adultery, but a blotchy John Bull says that although he deserves them he is not going to be allowed to claim them. Between them, a principal witness, Majocchi, is getting a bloody nose. Soldiers and sailors are cheering. There were popular demonstrations in favour of Caroline: five thousand seamen paraded to her house and an attempted mutiny in a battalion of the guards rattled Wellington, who wrote, 'In one of the most critical moments that ever occurred in this country we and the public have reason to doubt in the fidelity of the troops – the only security we have not only against revolution but the life and property of every individual.'

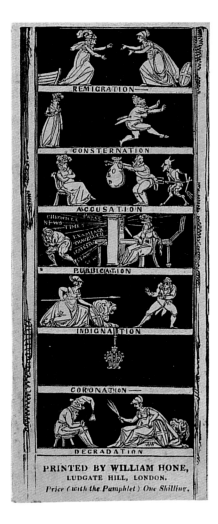

## The Radical Ladder

October 1820

GEORGE CRUIKSHANK

*In the pamphlet* The Queen's Matrimonial Ladder, *in August, Cruikshank had taken the side of the Queen, but here he attacks her as a leader of revolutionaries who will overturn the whole constitution of the country – Commons, Lords and King. The Jacobins are sheltering under her long cloak. The rungs of the ladder are Spa Fields Riot, Smithfield, Hunt's Procession, Peterloo and Cato Street, leading to mob government, revolution, anarchy and ruin. The message is clear: Caroline is being used by revolutionary forces – the wheel is slowly beginning to turn. This appeared in a pamphlet commissioned by the pro-George Loyalist Association.*

## The Queen's Matrimonial Ladder

1820

GEORGE CRUIKSHANK

*Hone, the radical publisher, passing a shop near Pentonville saw a toy – the Matrimonial Ladder – that inspired him to devise a chronicle of George's rise and fall. Cruikshank's one-inch-high scenes depict George's progress on the steeple ladder, rising from Qualification – even then he was drunk – to the high point of Caroline's departure, Emigration, and then down to Degradation, where as a dunce he is about to be birched by Britannia. The print was sold with a pamphlet of the same name for a shilling, and went into dozens of editions. In the autumn of 1820, when new, spicy details appeared daily, Hone used to meet Cruikshank, and occasionally William Hazlitt, in the Southampton Coffee House in Chancery Lane to plan their next attack on the monarch.*

### The Royal Extinguisher, or, The King of Brobdingnag & the Lilliputians

7 April 1821

GEORGE CRUIKSHANK

On 23 January George made a speech in which he confirmed the offer of a parliamentary grant of £50,000 a year to Caroline. This was the turning point in the whole crisis. The popularity of the Queen had been fading and George seized the opportunity to renew the very generous offer she had turned down in June 1820, but which she now accepted. Although she had forced the Government to climb down, her reputation had been ruined and neither the Government nor the people would ever accept her as Queen. Lord Liverpool, looking like an imbecile, can hardly believe his luck.

## THE BEGGAR's PETITION.

### The Beggar's Petition

August 1820

ISAAC CRUICKSHANK

*Caroline had just moved from Mrs Wood's house in South Audley Street – her first place of refuge – to Bradenburg House, a palatial house on the Thames at Hammersmith. This print, and the broadside that accompanies it, yellowed with age, depicts George as a beggar seeking reconciliation with his wife. This incident is entirely apocryphal because George never considered it for a moment, but it shows the moral high ground that Caroline had won just before her trial started.*

> *Pity the sorrows of a poor old man,*
> *Whose worn-out limbs have borne him to your door;*
> *My case is dwindl'd to the shortest span –*
> *Oh! let me in, and I will ask no more?*
>
> *Oh wife! sweet soother of my care,*
> *Kill not with anguish by your stern decree;*
> *I ling'ring fall a victim to despair,*
> *Scorn'd by the World, by Justice, and by Thee.'*

### My Ass in a Band-box

May 1821

WILLIAMS

*In January 1821 Theodore Lane had produced a coarse image of Caroline indecently dressed and sitting on a zebra in a bandbox. This is the counter-blast showing George as a Roman emperor – not caricatured – sitting on Lord Conyngham, who had just been appointed Groom of the Bedchamber and Master of the Robes. The cuckold's horns are in the basket and the bandbox, which contains muffs, implies the flow of gifts to the Conynghams. This is one of the last sharply satirical attacks over the divorce saga as Caroline had accepted defeat; the coronation was a month away; and a month later she was to die.*

*The, My Ass in a Band-box.*

August 1821

WILLIAMS

*This is how George was seen as responding to the news of Caroline's death:*

> *Oh! What pleasures will abound,*
> *Now my wife is laid in ground.*

### Coronation Banquet, Westminster Hall

1824

W. J. BENNETT AFTER CHARLES WILD

*After the crowning ceremony in the Abbey on
19 July 1821, George processed to Westminster
Hall on a walkway that had been raised so
the people could see him. He was preceded by
young aristocratic ladies – the debutantes of
their day – scattering rose petals in his path.
The coronation banquet was a gargantuan feast
provided by 23 kitchens which produced 160
tureens of soup; fish, venison, mutton, veal,
with gravy in 460 sauceboats; 9840 bottles of
wines and 100 gallons of iced punch.*

*During the first course the King's Champion,
an appointment which went back to Norman
times, entered Westminster Hall on a horse to
a flourish of trumpets, which may have caused
the horse to defecate. On his right was the Earl
Marshall, Lord Howard of Effingham, and
on his left the High Constable, the Duke of
Wellington. They rode to the steps where
George sat on a throne. A herald read out the
challenge of the Champion who offered to fight
anyone who questioned the King's title, and his
gauntlet was thrown down three times. George
drank to his Champion from a silver cup which
he was given to keep as his fee. Then the three
riders had to back their horses out of the hall,
a very difficult manoeuvre.*

*The ceremonies in both the Abbey and
Westminster Hall were dramatic recreations
of medieval ceremonies, and Walter Scott, the
novelist, gloried in 'the rich spectacle of the
aisles crowded with many plumage, coronets,
and caps of honour, and the sun…which
catched as it passed the glittering folds of a
banner, or the edge of a group of battleaxes.'
No succeeding monarch ever dared to replicate
this extravaganza.*

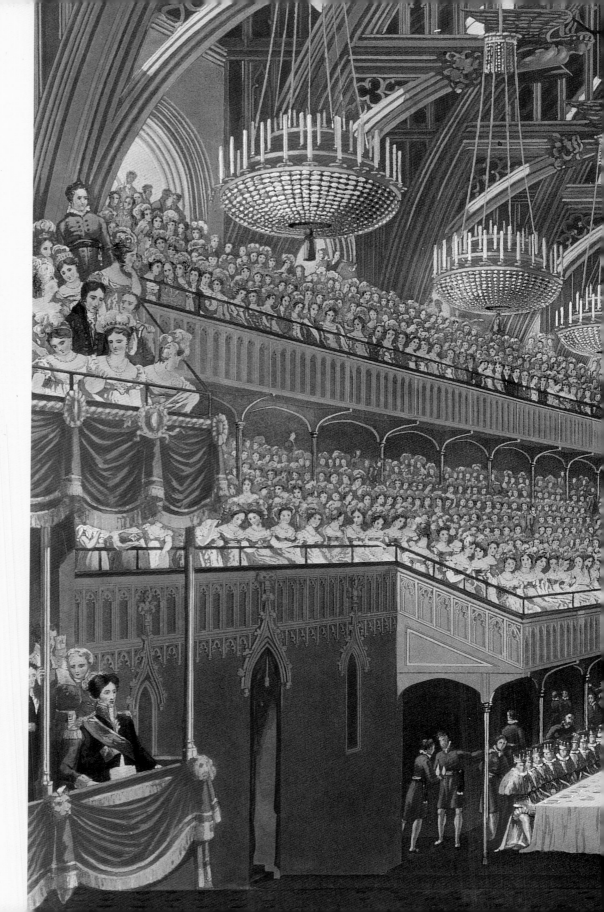

# 16 King at Last

BY THE TIME George ascended the throne the power of the Crown had been significantly circumscribed and reduced. Political power now rested with the Prime Minister, supported by his Cabinet, and dependent upon sustaining a majority in the House of Commons and hopefully in the House of Lords.

During the years up to George III's decline into senility and during the Regency itself, the government of the country lay in the hands of ministers. George III was the last British monarch to dismiss a government of which he did not approve; George IV might well have liked to do so but could never summon up the energy. Lord Liverpool had been Prime Minister for a total of eight years of his Regency and George did not dismiss him on becoming monarch, despite their an uneasy relationship. George did not disguise his disgruntlement – he was openly rude to Liverpool in front of his ministers and so openly critical behind his back that Wellington once bluntly asked, 'If you do not like us, why do you not turn us out?' The King merely bowed.

The disputes between them were principally about patronage. Liverpool, with the support of his Cabinet, would not approve the appointment of Lord Conyngham as Lord Steward of the Household. He also successfully objected to the appointment of one of George's friends to the deanery at Windsor. However, Liverpool had become indispensable: there was no alternative and that did not improve the relationship between Prime Minister and King.

One Tory whom George could not stand was George Canning. He had resigned over the Queen's trial and there had been a long-running rumour that he was one of Caroline's paramours. In 1799 Canning had visited Caroline at Blackheath, and she seems to have encouraged him to flirt; but in the same month he met and fell in love with Joan Scott. She was an heiress, and he needed money, so he was not going to endanger either those prospects or his political reputation by becoming entangled with the Princess of Wales. George IV knew this history, and told him later that in the Delicate Investigation he had himself struck out Canning's name. Happily married to the heiress, Canning was an example of domestic virtue – very different from his ministerial colleague in Parliament, Palmerston,

who had fathered four illegitimate children by the age of forty. Canning was devoted to his children and glad that Caroline consented to be godmother to their eldest son.

George's resentment towards Canning arose from his resignation from the Government in December 1820 on the grounds that he could not agree, after the collapse of Caroline's trial, that her name should continue to be excluded from the liturgy. Neither the Government nor the King would budge and so he resigned: an act that seemed to open the old question of whether he had once been Caroline's lover. The King resisted attempts by Liverpool to bring Canning back into the Cabinet. Canning came to accept that he would not return to front-line politics and he decided to accept the Governor-Generalship of India (a post that would also give some relief to his pressed financial position). The dramatic suicide of Castlereagh, his long-time rival, in August 1822, changed everything. Liverpool desperately needed Canning to be the Government's main spokesman in the Commons and Canning was flattered to have a pivotal role in the Cabinet. But the King continued to resist (which almost led to Liverpool resigning) until Wellington told him there was no alternative but to have Canning back.

They clashed again in 1824 after a number of colonies in Latin America successfully rebelled against the Spanish crown. Canning, with the support of the Cabinet, agreed to recognize the new revolutionary governments at Buenos Aires, and in Mexico and Colombia. George was so peeved that he refused to read the King's Speech to Parliament, claiming that his gout was too bad and he had lost his false teeth.

A recurring problem for the Government was getting the King to deal with official business. In 1822 George persuaded Sir Benjamin Bloomfield, his Private Secretary, to retire and in his place he appointed a surgeon, Sir William Knighton. It was a strange relationship, which has been described by one of George's biographers as that of 'an exasperated governess and a wayward charge'. But the great value of Knighton, as far as the Government was concerned, was that he was able to persuade the King to see Government papers and to sign them.

In 1825 George's hostility to Canning suddenly ended. Intuitively George had come to recognize that Canning was not only

A LEAP YEAR Drawing Room, or the pleasures of petticoat Government?

**A Leap Year Drawing Room, or, The Pleasures of Petticoat Government?**

June 1820

WILLIAM BENBOW

In this extravagant display of rampant feminism George is surrounded only by women. Isabella Hertford kisses his hand and Lady Conyngham waits to receive the booty due to a royal favourite, carrying a bag marked 'The Receiver General'. This is not an attack upon George's effeminacy but the influence of his paramours – there was much speculation on these lines when he became King.

NECESSITAS NON HABET LEGES, — or — the Nauseous Pill.

### Necessitas Non Habet Leges, or, The Nauseous Pill

10 February 1823

WILLIAMS

*After Castlereagh's suicide George reluctantly took Liverpool's advice and appointed Canning Foreign Secretary, from the left of the Tory Party. George behaved as a constitutional monarch should. Here he is having to swallow Canning's appointment and plaintively hopes that Canning will follow Castlereagh's policies – a proposal Canning dismisses with 'What do you mean? To finish like him?' Liverpool observes, 'We are all obliged to swallow what we do not like at times,' while the ultra-Tory Eldon, behind the screen, urges him to reject the appointment. The Tory Party was widely split, but the underrated Liverpool held it together.*

the ablest minister in his Government but also the most popular – a popularity won as the first statesman to make public speeches around the country, something that was alien to Tory practice and therefore a source of Tory suspicion. He was also aware that Canning assiduously courted the press – he was the first leading politician to realize the importance of public opinion. George invited Canning to attend him more frequently. The minister responded by sending more Foreign Office papers to the King, who disbanded his coterie of foreign ambassadors and let Canning see the reports he received from Hanover (which proved to be more valuable than the reports of the English ambassadors). Canning also helped George by despatching to the Embassy in Buenos Aires one of Lady Conyngham's former lovers, who was about to return to London. The George–Canning relationship flourished – there was a mutual congeniality.

When in February 1827 Liverpool, in his fifty-eighth year, had a paralytic stroke, George was deprived of a man who had held the Government together for fifteen tumultuous years. It was a difficult act to follow. Liverpool had intended Canning to

be his successor and George was happy to accept him as the front runner, but the Tory Party was hopelessly split on three issues – Catholic emancipation, the Corn Laws, and Canning's foreign policy. George first suggested that the Cabinet should elect their own leader – a proposal rejected by Peel as unconstitutional – and it soon became clear that the ultra-Tory Protestants could not themselves form a government. George IV was scrupulous in trying to get the leading Tories to agree but Eldon would not serve under Peel; Wellington and Peel would not serve under Canning; and Canning would not serve under either Wellington or Peel. Too many Tories had been wounded by Canning's witty sarcasm and there was a feeling among the Tory aristocrats that he was being 'too clever by half' (a similar fate befell Iain Macleod in the 1960s). A cabal of rebel Tory peers opposed to Canning, led by the Duke of Rutland, made George very resentful, and when the King eventually gave Rutland an audience George skilfully turned the conversation off the subject and round to a picture of Maria, The Oaks filly.

On 4 April he asked Canning to draw up proposals for a new administration but he insisted that the Cabinet had to have a

## A Complete Turn-out Among the Cabinet-makers

April 1827

H. HEATH

Liverpool had a stroke in February, but it was not until April that George ordered Canning to form a government. Several leading Tories, including Wellington, Peel and Eldon, resigned – the event that this print records. George confidently says, 'We can do without you.' The caption at the bottom begins: 'A turn-out took place on the first of April in the above Shop in consequence of the Master taking on a new and clever foreman who however is not in very high favour with the refractory workmen.' High Tories were not popular and their departure was welcomed in the press.

THE FUNERAL OF TORY-PRINCIPLE.
*Dutifully Dedicated to the HOLY ALLIANCE.*

## The Funeral of Tory Principle

April 1827

H. B. [JOHN DOYLE]

*This eloquently records the resignation of the leading right-wing Tories who could not accept Canning, the liberal Tory, as Prime Minister because he was in favour of Catholic emancipation. The leading mourner is Wellington who, within two years, was to be viciously attacked by several of the other mourners for his volte-face.*

Protestant majority. Wellington, Peel and five other Cabinet ministers resigned immediately and so Canning had to count upon several Whigs joining his administration. The Tory resignations only confirmed to George his choice. Canning reported the conversation that he had with the King: 'Sir, your father broke the domination of the Whigs, I hope your Majesty will not endure that of the Tories,' to which George replied, 'Well if you are not frightened, I am not.'

It was agreed that ministers should be allowed their own views on Catholic emancipation, which was a step towards reform, but they were resolutely opposed to any measure of parliamentary reform. On this compromise Canning's Government was established, but it was only his force of character that held it together. When Canning unexpectedly died in August, in the very same room in Chiswick House in which Fox had died, there was no one who could hold this strange coalition together.

George appointed Goderich, a former Chancellor of the Exchequer, who was to become one of the most unsuccessful English Prime Ministers. Affable and honourable, he was also weak and indecisive. On one occasion, overcome by the recent death of one of his daughters, and the impossible task of controlling his ministers, he broke down and wept – which earned him George's condemnation as 'a blubbering fool'. However, George had a hand in his downfall, having insisted that he appoint one of the King's friends as Chancellor of the Exchequer (in the expectation that he would be more helpful over the King's debts). In January 1828 Goderich finally resigned.

George had to send for Wellington, who was shown into the King's bedroom, where he found George wearing a dirty silk jacket and a grubby turban night-cap, to be told that he was to become Prime Minister. George's only requests were that Grey should not to be invited to join the Cabinet and that he did not expect his new Government to do much, or indeed anything, on Catholic emancipation. George may well have felt safe in that, since emancipation was the issue on which Wellington had refused to serve Canning.

**The Three Georges – the Patron – the Sovereign – and the Patriot**

7 May 1827

C. WILLIAMS

*This print shows the popularity of the King's decision to appoint Canning Prime Minister. George, together with St George and Canning, slays the seven-headed Hydra of Tory ministers who had resigned. For some weeks the press was strongly pro-Canning and George was praised for listening to the voice of the people, even by the Radical Fairburn, who published this print.*

**Cottage Amusement**

12 February 1828

H. HEATH

This print records the fall of Goderich's administration in January 1828. He is the dead pin at the bottom left. Only Wellington remains standing; he had been appointed Prime Minister in January. Lady Conyngham is implicated as instrumental in the appointment of Wellington, but there is no evidence to support this. On the right her son tells his mother to support Wellington because of his help in securing him a promotion. More presciently, on the left an Irishman asks for Catholic emancipation.

## A Change in the Head of Affairs

January 1828

WILLIAM HEATH

*A play on words. Goderich resigned as Prime Minister on 8 January 1828 and the King surrenders his 'wig' to Wellington, who receives it saying, 'Happy I am to see the Whig discarded.' This is not quite right as George received Wellington in his bed saying, 'Arthur, the Government is defunct.'*

## A Political Reflection

February 1828

WILLIAM HEATH

*This eloquent comment appeared within a few days of Wellington becoming Prime Minister. George once again is depicted as a baby in a cradle, attended by Lady Conyngham who uses her influence to support the Iron Duke.*

# 17 King Arthur

WELLINGTON, THE IRON DUKE, was, above all, a pragmatist and only secondly a Protestant. On 19 July 1828 Daniel O'Connell won a by-election in County Clare, but as a Catholic he was not able to take his seat in the House of Commons. Wellington realized this situation would probably make Ireland ungovernable. Catholic emancipation had been debated on several occasions in the House of Commons, where it had received a small majority, but the House of Lords was implacably opposed, and the King, as head of the Church of England, was likely to oppose any change – just as his father had done.

Wellington expected his Cabinet to obey him just as his armies had, and so he was much put out when they said he could not hold the two jobs of Prime Minister and Commander-in-Chief. However, they did unite in support of his efforts to persuade the King during the summer and autumn of 1828 that a measure of Catholic relief was necessary in order to prevent turmoil in Ireland. The King allowed the Cabinet to discuss the matter, thus removing the embargo that George III had insisted upon in 1807. The Cabinet soon agreed a Catholic Relief Bill.

Wellington learnt that the Duke of Cumberland, who had been living in Berlin, was going to lead the Protestant opposition and so he asked him not to return to England. This only confirmed to Cumberland that it was his duty to do exactly that, and he arrived back at Windsor in January 1829. He set about persuading his brother not to give his assent to any Act that relieved the exclusions on Catholics. The Lord Privy Seal, Ellenborough, believed that 'the King is afraid of him'. Certainly Cumberland was capable of working his brother up to a state of frenzy in which the King talked for hours on end and became steadily angrier. There was a rumour that Cumberland was organizing a huge mob of 20,000 Protestants to march on Windsor to demand no concessions. Wellington hoped he would actually do this as he could then have arrested him for treason and put him in the Tower of London.

On 26 February Wellington presented an ultimatum to the King: if Cumberland did not leave the country the Government would resign. There was a five-hour audience, which was lachrymose at times. On 4 March Wellington, Peel and Lyndhurst saw the King for a further five hours, during which they submitted their resignations, which he accepted. However,

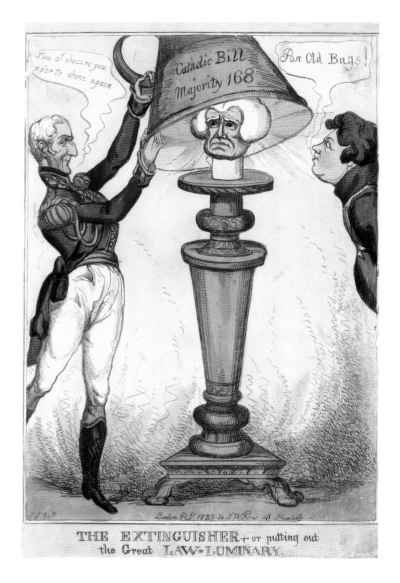

**The Extinguisher, or, Putting Out the Great Law-Luminary**

1829

THOMAS JONES

*On its first reading in the Commons the Catholic Relief Bill of 1829 had a majority of 178; on its second reading 180; and 178 on its third reading on 30 March (168 shown in the print is wrong). Majorities in the Lords were 105 and 109. Wellington had triumphed and here he snuffs out Eldon – Old Bags – the ultra Protestant.*

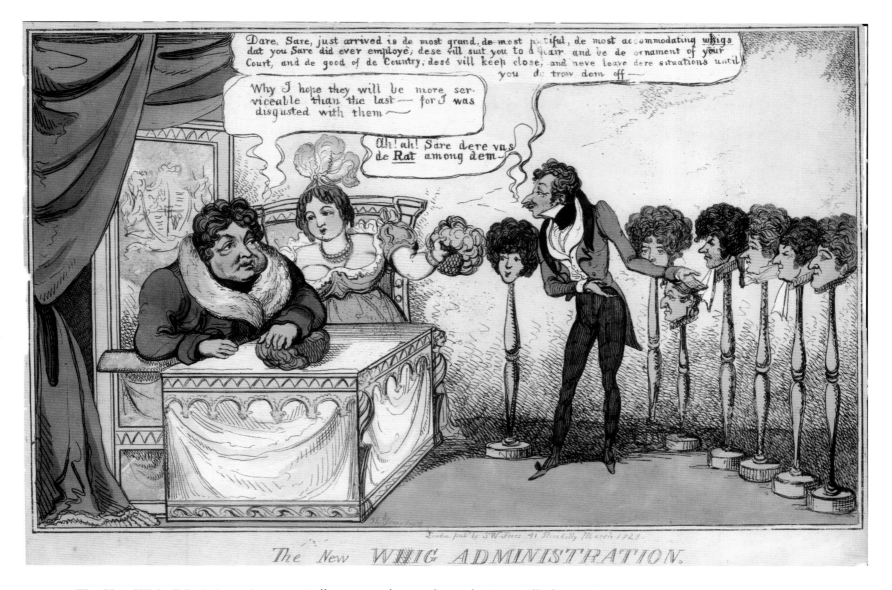

**The New Whig Administration**

March 1828

THOMAS JONES

*Following a cabinet split on the Corn Bill, the remaining Canningites were on the verge of resigning (and actually resigned two months later). George momentarily examines the possiblity of the return of the Whigs, but it was never a serious likelihood.*

before he went to bed that night George had a change of heart. He decided that he could not do without Wellington and he wrote to him:

My dear friend, as I find the country would be left without an administration, I have decided to yield my opinion to that which is considered by the Cabinet to be for the immediate interests of the country. Under the circumstances you have my consent to proceed as you propose with the measure.  God knows what pain it causes me to write these words. G.R.

On 13 April 1829 George IV gave his consent to the Catholic Relief Bill, saying that Wellington was 'King Arthur', O'Connell was 'King of Ireland', and he was 'Canon of Windsor'.

George felt that the Tory Party – the very party on which his father had depended upon for most of his reign – had ratted on this major issue of principle. He could have abdicated and gone to his other kingdom, Hanover, which he frequently threatened to do, but George was just too old and too comfortable to start life all over again at sixty-six. He made the best decision, both for himself and his country.

**Finis**

April 1829

WILLIAM HEATH

*There was some speculation before the commission appeared in his presence that the King would refuse to sign the Catholic Relief Bill. Peel, who is on his knees receiving the signed Act, said that the actual signing was 'the last and most difficult stage'. Wellington conceals from the King the image of his father, George III.*

**My Father's Ghost, or,
A Voice from the Grave**

April 1829

WILLIAMS(?)

On 13 April the King had given his assent to the Catholic
Relief Bill, returning it with the comment, 'The King never
before affixed his name with pain or regret, to any act of
the Legislature'. As a mitre falls from George's head the
apparition of his father appears, saying, 'Stop – and hear me!'
On many occasions the King had said that he was betraying
the constitution, his coronation oath, and his father's memory,
such was the grip that George III still held over his son.

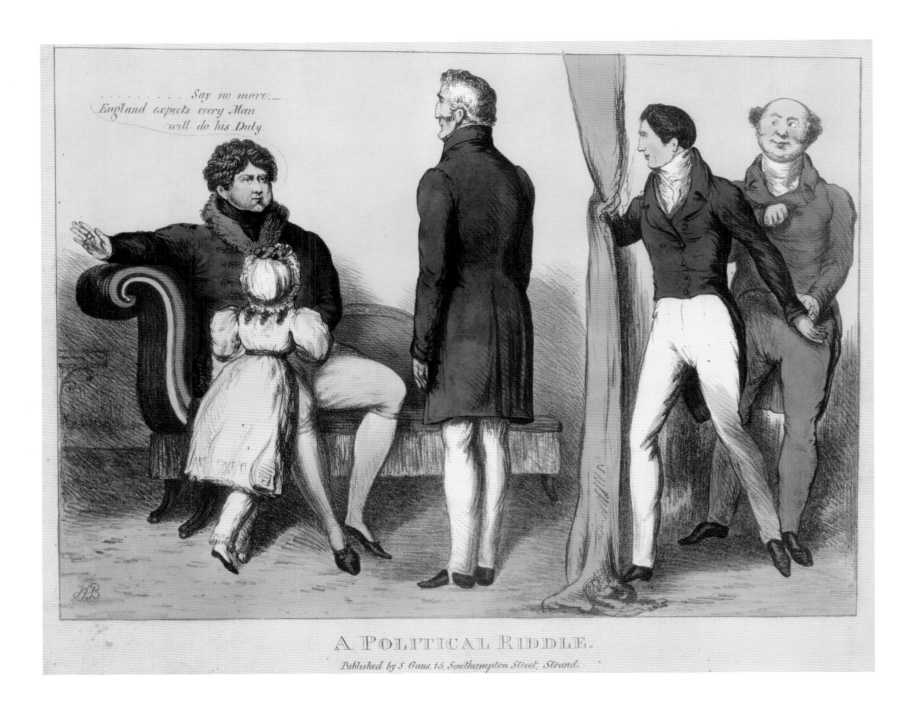

## A Political Riddle

6 June 1829

H. B. [JOHN DOYLE]

*This is a good example of the King following Wellington's advice when his instincts may have preferred something else. The issue was whether the British Government should intervene in the coup in Portugal, where Don Miguel had seized power and ousted the royal family. The very young Portuguese Princess had come to England to rally the royalists and George treated her kindly. However, Wellington did not want to become involved again in Peninsular politics, and in spite of strong Opposition pressure he maintained a policy of neutrality, which George accepted.*

## An Eclipse Lately Discovered in the Georgium Sidus, and Quite Unexpected by Any of the Astronomers

June 1829

A. SHARPSHOOTER

*The ultra-Tory press and some caricatures attacked Wellington for pushing through Catholic emancipation. This print shows an angry and glaring Wellington, who has not eclipsed the radiant serenity of George.*

A. Sharpshooter fec.                                    London: Pub. by J.W. Fores, 41, Piccadilly, 1829

AN ECLIPSE

Lately discoverd in the Georgium Sidus, and quite unexpected by any of the Astronomers.

## The Steam King

3 August 1829

*This rare print unusually uses one of the newfangled machines of the Industrial Revolution to emphasize Wellington's power. The Prime Minister, assisted by Peel, prints off Parliamentary Bills, especially those associated with Catholic emancipation. The King is the source of the power that drives the machine, although he is blindfolded. Lady Conyngham stokes the furnace with some of his baubles while Eldon, the arch-Tory, and a bishop tell her not to overdo it, otherwise the King will burst and blow them all up.*

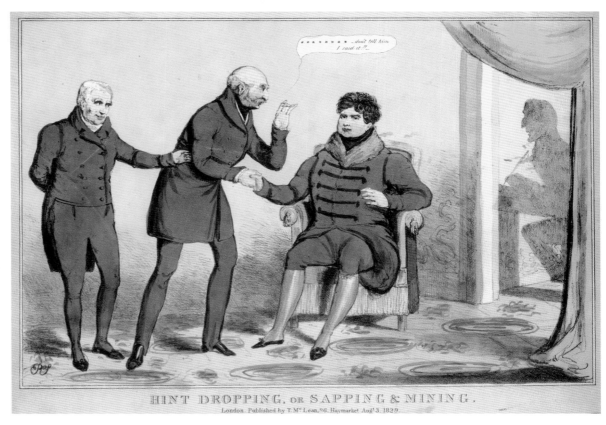

HINT DROPPING, or SAPPING & MINING.

London. Published by T. McLean, 26, Haymarket Augt 3. 1829.

## Hint Dropping, or, Sapping and Mining

3 August 1829

ROBERT SEYMOUR

*The Duke of Cumberland, having failed to stop his brother giving assent to the Catholic Relief Bill, devoted his conspiratorial powers to trying to drive Wellington out of office. He is assisted here by Eldon, but the shadow behind the curtain saw them off.*

## 18 Going Downhill

FROM HIS YOUTH George consumed enormous quantities of food and drink. Just before the King's death in 1830 the Duke of Wellington confided to Mrs Arbuthnot his amazement at the amount the King had consumed one evening after going to bed: 'two glasses of hot ale and toast, three glasses of claret, some strawberries!! and a glass of brandy.' A month later Wellington saw him consume a breakfast of 'Pidgeon and Beef Steak Pye, of which he ate two Pigeons and three Beefsteaks, three parts of a bottle of Mozelle, a Glass of Dry Champagne, two Glasses of Port, and a Glass of Brandy.'

Such an appetite had been achieved only through decades of enthusiastic and regular devotion to his stomach. In 1799 the artist Joseph Farington recorded that the Prince of Wales drank half-pint measures of gin and water, and by the time of his accession in 1820 he had added to this copious quantities of whisky. His favourite tipples were a sweet cherry liqueur known as maraschino, and curaçao. At Princess Charlotte's sixteenth-birthday party the Prince got so drunk and he abused Grey and Grenville so much that Charlotte broke down in tears and had to be led away by Sheridan. George was too ill to attend his daughter's funeral.

As a result of the 1703 Methuen Treaty wines from Portugal came into England with little or no duty: the aristocracy quickly took up the habit of drinking port, which inflames any arthritic condition, and George's daily consumption of port and brandy led to his suffering from gout at an early age. Gout stools were designed to give the sufferer some relief from the agonizing pain and by 1826 the King's bed had no fewer than 'eleven gouty pillows'.

Throughout his life George was not only overweight but often overwrought. He was seriously ill in 1786, 1787, 1791, 1797, 1800, 1804, 1811, 1814, 1820, 1823 and 1827. The symptoms – violent cramps and spasms, bilious attacks, headaches, stiffness in the arms and hands, swollen legs, sores and rashes – were probably caused by the family complaint, variegate porphyria. In 1820 he complained to his brother Frederick about 'the gout flying about me'.

The main treatment was the long-established practice of bloodletting. He first experienced this in the early 1780s and during his life George not only got used to it but rather welcomed it: on some occasions he bled himself, referring to it occasionally as 'a sport'. A doctor in 1813 reported that he saw twenty ounces of blood being taken from George whereas it was dangerous to exceed taking more than eight ounces at a time, and on another occasion seventeen leeches were stuck on one of his knees. (Bloodletting, also known as phlebotomy, has been revived today to deal with the genetic disorder haemochromatosis, which is the build up of too much iron in the body, the symptoms of which are unexplained fatigue, lethargy and pain. It may well be that George also suffered from this and got genuine relief from the bloodletting.) The other, harsh remedy was cupping: a 'cure' that involved raising blisters on the back and buttocks by the application of hot glasses so that harmful humours could escape from the body. During his life George was cupped hundreds of times.

George's increase in weight was recorded not only by himself but also in many memoirs. In 1809 Lady Bessborough, fighting off a clumsy grope, described him as 'that immense grotesque figure flouncing about half on the couch, half on the ground'. In 1810 Benjamin West, the painter, noted that 'George has grown

### The Sick Prince

16 June 1787

JAMES GILLRAY

*When Maria Fitzherbert refused to see George following Fox's denial of their marriage, he took to his bed – one of his favourite amorous ruses. He was said to be in great danger… so his recovery was miraculous! The Prince dreams of greatness to come, in the year 1800, while Time, with his scythe, advances. Pitt and friends, on the right, have daggers at the ready as Fox prays for his deliverance. Throughout his life George suffered from bouts of illness. Horace Walpole thought he was 'deeply afflicted with the scrofulous humour which the Princess of Wales had brought into the blood.' He was one of nature's hypochondriacs, but these bouts of illness were occasioned by stress and aggravated by his growing addiction to laudanum – an alcoholic tincture of opium.*

The SICK PRINCE.

Pub.d June 16, 1787. by S.W. Fores. N.o 3 Piccadilly.

## Princely Agility, or, The Sprained Ankle

January 1812

GEORGE CRUIKSHANK

*In November, George had sprained his ankle teaching Charlotte how to do the Highland Fling. Such was his general health that even the smallest incident laid him low. Rumours circulated that, like his father, he was becoming insane. On this occasion his doctors prescribed large doses of laudanum – as much as one hundred drops every three hours. George was well on the way to becoming an addict.*

enormously large, a figure like Henry VIII.' In 1812 it was the sculptor Nollekens: 'Your Royal Highness has increased in fullness of face the thickness of two fingers since I first modelled your face.' The expansion of girth was relentless. Records show that his jackets and waistcoats had to be let out; that in 1821 he needed a whalebone corset; and his weight increased from seventeen stone to twenty-two stone in the year of his death, when his stomach reached his knees, and his cousin and brother-in-law, the Duke of Gloucester, said that his body was like 'a feather bed'.

In January 1823, George was reported as suffering from rheumatic gout that was so bad he was 'hardly able to turn in bed without screaming'. He took to his bed for a month in March 1823 and Wellington thought he would not last the next six months.

**Consultation on the Best Cure for the Gout
i.e. – Multum in Parvo!**

August 1816

George's overinflated hand protects the overinflated army
budget, which had not been cut after Wellington's victory a
year earlier. The Whigs, led by Brougham, had attacked the
Regent, who desired the House of Commons 'to lavish on their
favourite the money extracted from the suffering people.' John
Bull's advice is to eliminate corruption, which will reduce the
swelling. This print is an interesting and rare example, showing
George's gout spreading to the rest of his body. A royal doctor
recorded that three of his fingers were completely numb and
useless. George complained that his 'poor right paw' could
hardly hold a pen and he had the 'greatest pain and difficulty
in writing, having the gout all over him but particularly in
both his hands'. By 1828 the gout had spread to his right arm,
making his right hand double in size – his valet had difficulty
getting his arm into the sleeve of his coat.

George's last night is well recorded. At half past eleven on 25 June 1830 he went to his bed, where one of his doctors, Sir Wathen Waller, sat up with him. He woke at two o'clock, had some clove tea and used his night-stool. He returned to his bed and asked for the windows to be opened. Another doctor, Sir Henry Halford, was summoned, and George, holding Waller's hand 'more strongly than usual', looked him full in the face and with 'an eager eye' exclaimed, 'My dear boy! This is death.' He sank back in his bed and breathed his last at quarter past three on 26 June 1830.

## A Fishing Party

27 June 1827

WILLIAM HEATH

*The political implication is that George is led by Lady Conyngham, singing Rule Britannia, and pushed along by Knighton as he goes fishing at Virginia Water. This early Zimmer frame emphasizes his corpulence and his near immobility – his waist was fifty inches around and he weighed over twenty stone.*

A FISHING PARTY, *What great enjoyments rise from trivial things ...*

## George IV's Death Chamber

1830

H. B. [JOHN DOYLE]

*This is a pencil drawing, held in the British Museum and never before reproduced, for a lithograph that did not appear. George IV reclines in a chair, his face hidden by a pillar (a convention for depicting distress, embarrassment or secrecy), attended by his doctor, Halford. Wellington and Cumberland push against the door to keep out the grinning skeleton of Death, armed with his customary spear, as they know that George's demise would also end their political power.*

# 19 George and the Press

THE FIRST DAILY LONDON NEWSPAPER appeared in 1702. By the 1780s, when George was in his late teens, there were over nine morning newspapers and ten evening papers. Others appeared weekly and there were several monthlies. Besides these, there was a growing number of provincial newspapers. George was always conscious of the criticisms of his behaviour that were made in the press and in satirical prints, and on several occasions he tried to suppress them.

In 1788 during the Regency Crisis the *Morning Post* started attacking the Prince by disclosing gossipy stories about Maria Fitzherbert. Richard Sheridan was given the task of buying-off the editor, John Benjafield, who was a blackmailer. Benjafield was quite prepared to pull a story after the subject had been forewarned and had paid for it not to appear. On this occasion, for a thousand guineas and an annuity he stopped attacking Maria and redirected his fire onto Pitt, extolling the virtues of the Prince – he had sold out to Carlton House.

In 1812 the *Morning Post* was still on side and, even after a St Patrick's Day dinner at which the Regent's name was hissed, it described him as 'the Glory of the People' and 'an Adonis of Loveliness'. This hyperbole was too much for the *Examiner*, which printed a piece by Leigh Hunt, the editor's brother, in which he pointed out the 'so-called Glory of the People' was in fact

> the subject of millions of shrugs and reproaches…this
> Adonis of Loveliness was a corpulent gentleman of fifty!
> In short, that this delightful, blissful, wise, pleasurable,
> honourable, virtuous, true and immortal Prince [was] a
> violator of his word, a libertine over head and ears in debt
> and disgrace, a despiser of domestic ties, the companion
> of gamblers and demireps, a man who has just closed half
> a century without one single claim on the gratitude of his
> country or the respect of posterity.

Both of the Hunt brothers were charged with the 'intention to traduce and vilify his Royal Highness, the Prince of Wales, Regent of the United Kingdom.' Although their defence was vigorously conducted by Henry Brougham, with a coruscating cross-examination, they were found guilty, fined £500 each and sentenced to two years in prison. This excessively hard sentence boomeranged back to the Regent, for Leigh Hunt became a hero

and his literary friends – Shelley, Keats, and Charles Lamb – all rounded on George.

George also had to withstand the withering attacks that came from two satirical magazines – the *Satirist* and the *Scourge*. The *Scourge*, first published in 1811, was 'A Monthly Expositor of Imposture and Folly'. Each copy contained a fold-out coloured plate. During the six years of this magazine's life George Cruikshank drew more than half of them, which established him as the major political cartoonist of the age. The plates were brutal, reckless, tasteless and bawdy. Their victims fart, vomit and excrete. In this rumbustious age all this quite happily existed alongside the elegance of beautiful furniture, ornamentation and high fashion. The *Scourge* and the *Satirist*

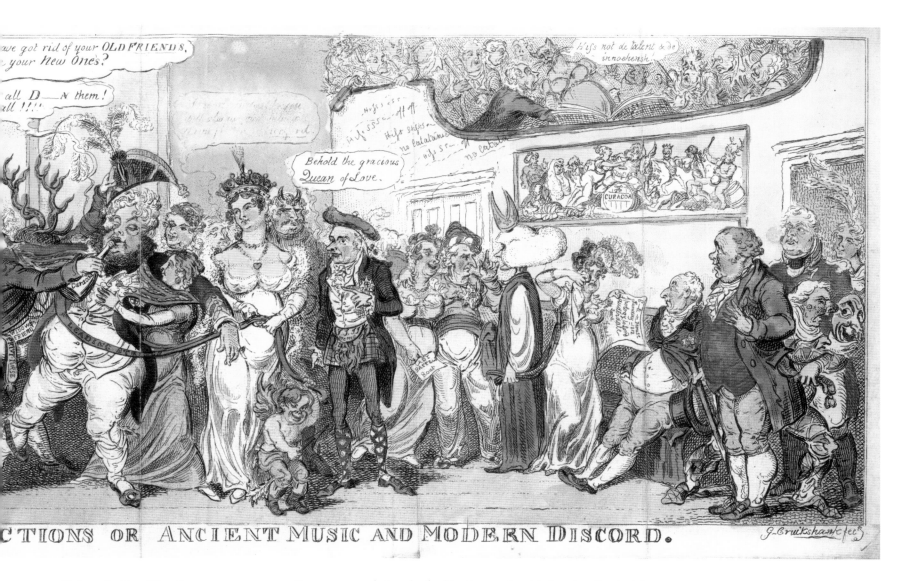

**Princely Predilections, or, Ancient Music and Modern Discord**

1 April 1812

GEORGE CRUIKSHANK

George sent a letter drafted by Perceval to his brother Frederick to justify his retention of the Tories in office, saying, 'I have no predilection to indulge nor resentment to gratify.' Cruikshank turned this phrase against him. When this print appeared in the Scourge it was laid before the Attorney General and the Solicitor General. Their judgment was that 'this is a most indecent and impudent print but it would require so much of difficult explanation stating it as a libel upon the regent that it does not appear to us advisable to make it the subject of a criminal prosecution.' So it was impossible to protect the public from seeing the Regent drunk, his fifty-two-year-old big-bosomed mistress, her cuckolded husband, and a leering cupid tickling her crotch with the tip of his wing.

were rivals. On one occasion the *Scourge* attacked three verse lampoons appearing in its competitor as

> they had obtained an extensive circulation among the lower orders…they render the names of our princes first familiar and then contemptible; they teach the peasant and the citizen to regard a court as a temple of debauchery, and the chief magistrate as a drunken profligate.

But as the *Scourge* was doing the same it reminds one of the blow and counterblow exchanged today between the *Sun* and *Daily Mirror*.

In 1820 George pressed 'Bags' Eldon, the Lord Chancellor, to prosecute the radical and licentious press and a law on ribaldry was considered. The *Loyalist* magazine in 1820 declared that unrest and riot were being stimulated by 'parodies, prints, caricatures, ribaldry, and ridicule'. A body called the Constitutional Association was set up to defend the Crown and in 1821 it prosecuted William Benbow over two obscene, libellous caricatures. But a Westminster jury declined to act on the indictment of a self-appointed association and an attempted prosecution of Hone's *Non mi ricordo!* also failed. London juries, to their great credit, would not be bent to the will of Carlton House.

Libel prosecutions also often rebounded on the Government. In 1824 John Hunt was charged for printing Byron's *The Vision of Judgement*, which attacked George III, but the court action meant that *The Times* reprinted the entire 848 lines of the lampoon. It was immediately picked up by the radical press, reprinted and sold widely. Hunt was fined only £100.

George liked collecting caricatures and from 1782 to 1830 he bought hundreds, having regular standing orders with printsellers. In the years 1806–7 he bought 121 caricatures from Hannah Humphrey alone. Percy Cruikshank recorded that Isaac and his son, George, had a way of sending a proof on the eve of publication, to the Prince:

> The plate being finished, a proof, in the shape of a roll of paper, was taken by a trusty agent, to Carlton House, at night. There a pair of sentries marched, in front of the Royal residence, and when their walk was back to back, the agent stepping up, unperceived, dropped the roll of paper over the open screen, in front of the House. This, in course of time, being found by [a] Royal porter, was opened, and after being enjoyed in the kitchen, was laid on the Royal breakfast table, and a very indigestible roll it must have provided.

*Which is the Dirtiest so foul the Stains will be Indelible*

### Which is the Dirtiest – So Foul the Stains Will Be Indelible

5 September 1820

WILLIAM HEATH

*For several years George and Caroline carried on their feud in the press, and far more fiercely than Prince Charles and Diana. Favourable stories, letters and rumours were leaked to their supporters. For Caroline it was* the Morning Chronicle, *the* Pilot *and from 1820* The Times. *The editor of the* Evening Star *turned down an offer of £300 a year to switch allegiance from the Princess to George. As she was the more popular it was more profitable for the newspaper to stick with her. George depended upon the* Morning Post *and the* Morning Herald.

His most gracious Majesty Hum IVth & his Ministers going to play the Devil with the Satirists

## His Most Gracious Majesty Hum IVth and his Ministers Going to Play the Devil with the Satirists

1820

George is determined to destroy the satirists even by discharging at them bombs from the great cannon he had been sent after the Napoleonic Wars. The satirists are depicted as troublesome gadflies whom Sidmouth, the Home Secretary, is trying to bring down with squirts from his doctor's clyster pipe. George, supported by Wellington, Liverpool and Castlereagh, says to Sidmouth, 'Here! Sid, you old tottering humbug, desire the Bishops to come along with a tinder box and matches...I tell you again I am King and be damned to you all, and I will do just as I please.' The ghost of George III appears, urging his son not to pursue the satirists through the courts, saying, 'Oh my Son! My dear Son if you prosecute them you will make their fortunes – but if you conduct yourself like a man and a gentleman you will destroy their profession.'

Don't talk to me of Radicals haven't I done
ev'ry thing in my power to promote the
good of the Parish – ever since I've
been in office – eh?

Mᴿ GEORGE KING – the PARISH OVERSEER

"And ratolorum too; and a gentleman born – who writes himself armigero, in any bill, warrant quittance
or obligato — Shakspeare"

Pub. June 1, 1829 by J. Gans, 13, Southampton St. Strand sole publisher of Paul Pry's Caricatures. None are original without his name

**Mr George King – the Parish Overseer**

1 June 1829

SHARPSHOOTER [PAUL PRY]

*This is one of a set of caricatures depicting the leading figures of the day as officials in a parish, rather like* Private Eye's *'parish letter' from the vicar of St Albion (Tony Blair). George, as the Overseer, says 'Don't talk to me of Radicals haven't I done ev'rything in my power to promote the good of the Parish – ever since I've been in office – eh?' The representation of George in his later years is much more benign and the quotation at the bottom is from* The Merry Wives of Windsor*: 'And ratolorum too; and a gentleman born – who writes himself armigero in any bill, warrant quittance or obligato.'*

George enjoyed laughing at others but drew a line at laughing at himself. When a particularly vicious cartoon appeared of himself or Lady Conyngham, Bloomfield, his Private Secretary, sent out Josh Calken, a bookseller in Pall Mall, to visit the publishers to try to prevent the print appearing, and in some cases to buy the copperplate, for as much as seventy guineas. However, George usually kept one print for himself – a superb collection that was sold in 1921 to the Library of Congress to raise more cash for George V to spend on his stamp collection!

George also turned to bribery. During the 1820s Lewis Marks was paid £500 to suppress various caricatures and poems, and in 1821 he received £45 for withdrawing one of Lady Conyngham winkling some gifts out of George. Marks did not stop at blackmail. He let the King's Private Secretary know that he was intending to publish a new poem called *Amoroso, King of Little Britain*: 'If you would be kind enough to call on me tomorrow morning I shall be glad as I shall not advertise it till I have your opinion on it.' Whether or not George stumped up this time is not recorded in the royal archives. George Cruikshank 'for a pledge not to caricature His Majesty in any immoral situation' received £100 – the receipt is in the Royal Library, Windsor. But that did not stop them.

Each prime minister from Pitt to Liverpool was concerned about the influence of the newspapers, and some leading politicians wanted them banned. In 1810 the anti-Jacobin *Revue* deplored the fact that alehouses were 'receptacles of vice' that displayed 'diabolical' Jacobin prints that promoted dissent and disobedience, and it urged magistrates to withhold licences from such publicans.

Through the period 1780 to 1830 every government paid, from its Secret Service funds, retainers to loyal newspapers. In the post-revolutionary early 1790s this amounted to £5,000 a year; if these payments ever flagged then the papers joined the opposition.

In the years 1819–22 alone the cost to the Treasury for such bribes amounted to £2,204.10 shillings (in today's money nearly £100,000). Satirical publications peaked in 1820, when 800 political caricatures appeared: the Treasury Solicitor considered 91 of them for prosecution, but decided against because juries would not convict and a trial merely gave oxygen to the satirical attack. Those 91 prints are still held today in the Treasury Solicitor's files in the National Archives.

The real fixer of the press for the Government was Charles Arbuthnot, Secretary to the Treasury – an earlier and less sophisticated version of modern-day spin doctors – whose job

## Head and Tail, or, A Crown Piece and a Sovereign

30 September 1829

WILLIAM HEATH

*This charming and rare print depicts George, flatteringly slim, as a gold sovereign, and the grossly overweight Lady Conyngham as the back of a five shilling piece. Above it is a quotation from* Henry VI – *'If thou be a King, where is thy Crown?' 'My Crown is in my heart, not on my head.'*

the immensely fat Lady Conyngham – the satirists were glad to focus on her girth rather than the King's. But the one passion George was not prepared to give up was his passion for building and rebuilding his houses and palaces, and reshaping the heart of London, and there are only a handful of prints on this.

Secondly, George had become more popular. His visits to Dublin and Edinburgh showed that many of his subjects liked him. By the middle of the 1820s, having overcome his suspicions of Canning he actually supported him, and was able to share in Canning's popularity.

Thirdly, the age of the separate satirical print was passing. George Cruikshank, the most biting satirist, found it easier to earn money by illustrating books – most notably Dickens's *Oliver Twist* – than drawing satirical sketches. The sharply cut lines of the copper-engraving were also giving way to the softer tones and shades of the lithograph. This time technology was on George's side, and right at the end of his reign Robert Seymour produced a lithograph in which a contented, pipe-smoking John Bull reassured the king that he really liked him.

was 'to get the press right'. In 1812 he considered buying a Sunday newspaper, the *News*, to counter criticism of George's treatment of Caroline, and in 1813 £300 was paid to the owner of the *Star* to turn against her. Alarmed by the radical press, Sidmouth, the Home Secretary, launched and funded the *White Dwarf* in 1817 to counter the subversive publication the *Black Dwarf*.

Other characters were more robust. Mrs Arbuthnot records that the Duke of Wellington 'passed half an hour laughing heartily with me at some caricatures of himself'. Wellington was very lucky as he was usually depicted as a strong man, not as a weakling or a womanizer. Just as Margaret Thatcher did not mind being portrayed as the Iron Lady, Wellington did not mind being portrayed as the Iron Duke. When the society courtesan Harriette Wilson advised Wellington that she would include him in her memoirs, he replied with the famous dismissal, 'Publish and be damned.'

The great wave of ridicule in 1820 surrounding the divorce ebbed quite quickly, and for the remaining nine years of his reign George was treated in a more kindly way. There were several reasons: first, George's behaviour was more restrained. There were no reports of drunkenness in public; he had long given up gambling; and he was content with one companion,

VOX POPULI, A GREAT PERSONAGE INCOG.

London. Published by T. McLean, 26, Haymarket. Nov: 21.1829

**Vox Populi**

21 November 1829

ROBERT SEYMOUR

This is an unusual print as it represents George as a popular
figure. George says hesitantly, 'I believe Mr Bull you are no
great admirer of His M....y?' The solid, pipe-smoking John
Bull replies, 'You are quite mistaken Sir, I only wished I liked
anyone about or belonging to him half so well.' This must
have gladdened George's heart.

# List of Characters

**Addington, Lord** (1757–1844) As Speaker of the House in 1801 he succeeded Pitt as Prime Minister. Negotiated the peace of Amiens with France but had to give way to Pitt in 1804. He was created Viscount Sidmouth in 1805. A regular member of successive Tory Governments, he was Home Secretary 1812–21. Following the Peterloo Massacre he introduced the savage laws restricting freedom. Always depicted with a clyster pipe, used for enemas, as his father had been a doctor.

**Arbuthnot, Charles** (1767–1850) A Tory MP and Secretary to the Treasury 1809–23. He would have remained in relative obscurity but for the fact that his wife Harriet, thought to be Wellington's mistress, left a full and frank diary of their great friendship with Wellington.

**Bergami, Bartolommeo**, sometimes spelt **Pergami**. Caroline's swarthy major domo who became her lover. He declined to attend her trial.

**Bloomfield, Benjamin** (1768–1846) A soldier whose skill at the cello, while posted to Brighton, was noticed by George, who made him his Chief Equerry. Private Secretary to George from 1817 until 1822 when he was dismissed. Disappointed not to receive a peerage.

**Blücher, Gebhard von** (1742–1819) Joined the Prussian Army at 18. Fought in the Seven Years War, the Polish War, and the French War (1793–94). Commander-in-Chief of Prussian Army in 1813. Beat Napoleon at Leipzig in 1813 and saved the day for Wellington at Waterloo. His soldiers nicknamed him 'Marschall Vorwärts' – he went mad before he died.

**Boyne, John** (1750–1810) An actor turned painter, engraver and publisher of caricatures. A fine draughtsman but a gentle satirist.

**Brougham, Lord** (1778–1868) A Whig MP from 1810. Defended Caroline at her trial and a constant thorn in the King's side. As Lord Chancellor 1830–34 he was one of the prime movers of the Reform Bill. Radical

throughout, he 'adopted' Cannes as his other home and put it on the tourist map.

**Brummell, George Bryan 'Beau'** (1778–1840) The leading dandy of his day, who had to leave England in 1816 because of his debts. Lived in Calais and Caen and died there in an asylum.

**Burke, Edmund** (1729–97) Politician, orator and philosopher. He was originally a Whig close to Fox and Sheridan, but they separated when his great work, *Reflections on the French Revolution* (1790), became one of the philosophical texts of Toryism. His support of Catholic emancipation meant he was often depicted in prints as a Jesuit or with a Catholic biretta.

**Canning, George** (1770–1827) A protégé of Pitt – orator, wit and poet. Prime Minister for six months in 1827. Most famous for his support in the 1820s of the South American countries which rejected Spanish rule: 'I called in the New World to redress the balance of the Old.'

**Caroline of Brunswick, later Princess of Wales** (1768–1821) Married George, a cousin, in 1795. They had a daughter, Charlotte, in 1796 but led completely separate lives. George tried to divorce her and brought a Bill of Pains and Penalties against her.

**Castlereagh, Lord** (1769–1822) Irish and English MP in the 1790s. Chief Secretary of Ireland 1798–1801 where he earned his reputation as a hard suppressor of rebellion – depicted with a cat of nine tails or a noose. Fought a duel with Canning in 1809. A key man in the Liverpool Government, he was Foreign Secretary and Leader of the House of Commons 1812–22. He cut his throat in August 1822.

**Charlotte, Queen** (1744–1818) She married George III at 17 and bore him 15 children. A plain, dull and dutiful wife who had a penchant for jewelry and snuff.

**Charlotte, Princess** (1796–1817) The only legitimate daughter of George. She refused to marry Prince William of Orange and married instead the almost penniless Prince Leopold of Saxe-Coburg-Saalfeld in 1816. She died giving birth to a stillborn son.

**Clarence, Duke of**, later **William IV** (1765–1837) George III third's son who was sent off to the Navy to serve in the West Indies. For 20 years he lived with the famous actress, Dorothea Jordan, who bore him nine children. Following Princess Charlotte's death he became second in succession and so he threw over Dorothea and married the austere Adelaide, but all their children died in infancy. He was always rather distant from George.

**Clarke, Mary-Ann** (1776–1852) The mistress of the Duke of York from 1803. In 1809, she was accused of selling commissions and the proceeds may well have ended up in the pocket of the financially embarrassed Duke of York.

**Cobbett, William** (1763–1835) After spells in the law and the army and a stay in America, he returned to Britain in 1800 and began the *Political Register* in 1802 to campaign for political reform. He became the leading radical journalist of his day, suffering vilification and imprisonment. Published *Rural Rides* in 1830.

**Conyngham, Lord** (1766–1832) Lord Steward of the Household 1821–30. Constable of Windsor Castle 1829–32. Famous for his wife becoming George's last mistress and companion. Invariably depicted in prints with cuckold horns.

**Conyngham, Lady** (1770–1861) George's last mistress – a woman of immense girth and immense greed.

**Creevey, Thomas** (1768–1838) A Liverpool merchant and Whig MP whose diary, not published until 1904, gives a good insight into Regency London.

**Cruikshank, Isaac** (1764–1811) A prolific artist who produced many prints – some striking, some routine. He died after a drinking bout.

**Cruikshank, George** (1792–1878) The son of Isaac, his first caricature was published at the age of 16. A brilliant political cartoonist from 1806 to 1821. He then became a major book illustrator, most famous for his depiction of Fagin in *Oliver Twist*. At first a rake, he abandoned drink becoming the Abstinence

Movement's greatest disciple. He is buried in St Paul's but this pillar of Victorian society managed to keep secret that he divided his life between two wives.

**Cumberland, The Duke of** (1771–1851) Fifth son of George III. Known as 'Wicked Ernest' – the prints were convinced he had murdered his valet, molested girls and fathered a child by his sister Sophia. He was an extreme Protestant who campaigned against his brother. Ended up as Elector of Hanover; Princess Victoria fortunately prevented him from becoming King of England.

**Curtis, Sir William** (1752–1829) MP for the City of London and Lord Mayor in 1795. A friend of George IV whom he accompanied to Scotland in 1822, where he added a certain absurdity to the whole visit.

**Dent, William** (fl. 1783–93) His caricatures in this ten-year period are very funny, vulgar and often obscene. Very much the working man's view of life. Nothing else is known about him.

**Doyle, John 'H.B.'** (1797–1868) His political caricatures first appeared in 1827 and depicted the political history of Britain for over 20 years. The use of lithography gave his images a soft look, and his portraits were not exaggerated. The vulgar derision of his predecessors was abandoned and his work paved the way to the gentility of *Punch*.

**Eldon, Lord** (1751–1838) Attorney General, then Lord Chief Justice and Lord Chancellor 1801–6 and 1807–27. A High Tory and leader of the Protestants against Catholic emancipation. The most reactionary Lord Chancellor of the 19th century.

**Fitzherbert, Mrs Maria** (1756–1837) She was a Roman Catholic and already twice widowed when George fell for her. Their marriage in 1785 was illegal and she bore her position and her eventual rejection with great dignity.

**Fox, Charles James** (1749–1806) The charismatic leader of the Whigs and the first Leader of the Opposition. Rose to fame by criticizing North's conduct of the American war but formed a coalition with him in 1782–83. Loathed by George III, he became the Prince of Wales's closest political friend and stood by him through the Mrs Fitzherbert scandal. His support of the French Revolution helped to keep the Whigs out of office. He was Foreign Secretary in the Ministry of All the Talents for a few months before his death.

**George III** (1738–1820) Succeeded his grandfather at the age of 22. Held to be partly responsible for the loss of the American colonies. Subject to fits of insanity brought on by the hereditary disease of porphyria. Morally strict, careful with money, scholarly, sensitive to the arts – he was transformed from being a figure of ridicule, 'Farmer George', to being the representative of the nation that took on Napoleon. Became permanently insane in 1811.

**Gillray, James** (1756–1815) The genius of British caricature. He first attacked Pitt and George III but following the horrors of the French Revolution he turned his brilliantly conceived satires against the Whigs, France and Napoleon. After 1807 his powers faded and in 1810 he went insane.

**Goderich, Viscount** (1782–1859) Tory Minister. President of the Board of Trade 1818–23; Chancellor of the Exchequer 1823–27; Prime Minister 1827–28. Could not stand the pressure and the pace. Cobbett nicknamed him 'Goody Goderich'.

**Grenville, Lord** (1759–1834) The Prime Minister of the Ministry of All the Talents, 1806–7. Renowned for his large bottom.

**Grey, Lord** (1764–1845) A leading Whig and briefly Foreign Secretary 1806–7, he advocated parliamentary reform from 1789 and became Prime Minister in 1830. He carried the Reform Bill of 1832. George IV had a strong personal antipathy to Grey, on account of his support for Caroline, and would not countenance his holding office.

**Halford, Sir Henry** (1766–1844) Physician to George III, George IV, William IV and Queen Victoria. He has much to answer for. Known as the 'Eel-backed baronet'. In 1809 his fees were £10,000 – roughly £300,000 today.

**Hangar, George** (1751–1824) A crony of George in his early years – either in a scrape or in debt.

**Heath, William** (1795–1840) From 1820 he produced a flood of political prints, some appearing under the name Paul Pry. He was described as 'the ex-captain of Dragoons, facile and profuse, unscrupulous and clever.' Henry Heath, another political caricaturist may have been his brother.

**Hertford, Lady** (1760–1834) Another of George's dominant older mistresses. From 1806 to 1820 she was very close to him and re-enforced his Tory instincts.

**Jersey, Lady** (1753–1821) George's mistress from 1793 to 1799 – she made sure that the marriage to Caroline took place to scotch Maria Fitzherbert. She also made sure the marriage could not succeed in order to secure her own position.

**Kent, Duke of** (1767–1820) George III's fourth son. Lived largely abroad but was the father of Victoria. He died when she was just eight months old.

**Knighton, Sir William** (1776–1836) A popular London doctor who was Wellington's physician in the Peninsula campaign, and from 1813 to the Prince of Wales, whose confidence he won. He was the King's Private Secretary and Keeper of the Privy Purse 1822–30. His influence over the King was due to some private papers that he had inherited from George's former Secretary, Sir John McMahon.

**Lawrence, Thomas** (1769–1830) Son of a West Country innkeeper whose talent was recognized while a child. ARA in 1791; RA in 1794; PRA in 1820. For over 20 years the most fashionable portrait painter in England.

**Leopold, Prince of Saxe-Coburg-Saalfeld** (1790–1865) A lucky man. He was virtually penniless when he married Princess Charlotte, who died within a year. In 1830 he declined the crown of Greece but in 1831 was elected King of the Belgians.

**Lieven, Princess de** (1785–1857) Married to the diplomat the Comte de Lieven, the Russian ambassador in London from 1812 to 1834. She was Metternich's mistress 1818–24 and was a major figure in the social and political life of London – she was really the ambassador.

**Liverpool, Lord** (1770–1828) Tory minister under Pitt, he later served as Foreign Secretary and was Prime Minister 1812–27. One of the least-known Prime Ministers, but a genius at holding the Tory Party together through turbulent times.

**Lyndhurst, Lord** (1772–1863) Lord Chancellor from 1827 to 1830 and again under Peel from 1841 to 1846. An opponent of reform whom the painter Benjamin Haydon described as 'a superannuated Mephistopheles'.

**McMahon, Colonel John** (1754–1817) The Prince of Wales's Private Secretary 1803–17. Red-faced and pimply he was known as 'The Privy Pimp'.

**Majocchi, Teodoro** Queen Caroline's personal servant who attested to her sleeping with Bergami in a tent on deck during her voyage to the Levant.

**Moira, The Earl of** (1754–1826) He fought in America (1775–80) and succeeded to the earldom in 1793. One of George's closest political friends. Later Governor-General of Bengal.

**Moore, Thomas** (1779–1852) Popular Irish poet and songwriter.

**Nash, John** (1752–1835) George appointed him Surveyor-General and Comptroller of the Office of Works in 1813. Thus started the partnership between King and architect which transformed the centre of London. He was also responsible for Regency stucco villas and the Brighton Pavilion.

**North, Lord** (1732–92) Prime Minister 1770–82. Held responsible for precipitating the Boston Tea Party in 1773, which led to the loss of the American colonies. He could not survive the defeat at Yorktown in 1781. He briefly shared power with Fox in the notorious coalition of opposites in 1783. Amiable, fat and witty, he was no war leader. Horace Walpole said of him: 'Though his country was ruined under his administration he preserved his good humour.'

**O'Connell, Daniel** (1775–1847) An Irish lawyer and advocate of Catholic emancipation. In 1823 he formed the Catholic Association and in 1828 was elected Member of Parliament for Clare. In 1830, following the passing of the Catholic Relief Act, he was able to take his seat in the House of Commons .

**Peel, Sir Robert** (1788–1850) Tory MP who earned the soubriquet 'Orange Peel' as Chief Secretary of Ireland 1812–18. He was Home Secretary 1822–27, giving his name to the new policemen – 'Peelers'. Leader of the Commons during the Catholic emancipation crisis 1828–30. Prime Minister 1834–35 and 1841–46. One of the great 19th-century statesmen, he twice managed to split the Tory Party. He died after a fall from his horse on Constitution Hill.

**Perceval, Spencer** (1782–1812) Tory Prime Minister 1809–12, he was assassinated by a madman as he entered the House of Commons. Known as 'Little P'.

**Pitt, William, the Younger** (1759–1806) Second son of the Earl of Chatham. Became Prime Minister in 1783 at the age of 24. He resigned in 1801 when George III refused to consider Catholic emancipation. Recalled to office in 1804. He died from drink in 1806.

**Portland, Duke of** (1738–1809) Prime Minister of the notorious Fox/North coalition for nine months from 1783. A leading Whig who went over to Pitt in 1794. Although deaf, gouty and infirm, he was recalled to be Prime Minister again from 1807 to 1809. Prints depict him as grey as Portland stone.

**Rowlandson, Thomas** (1756/7–1827) More famous for his watercolours of town and country life than his satirical work. His political caricatures were 'pot-boilers' – the best being of Napoleon, whom he loathed.

**Sayers, James** (1748–25) His active period was from 1781 to 1795 and his main target was Fox. His prints were heavily etched in black.

**Scott, Sir Walter** (1771–1832) The celebrated Scottish novelist who masterminded George's visit to Scotland in 1822.

**Shelburne, The Earl of** (1737–1805) Prime Minister for a few months in 1782–83, but he was distrusted as an intriguer, gaining the nickname 'Malagrida' after an infamous Jesuit plotter. Easily recognized in prints as swarthy, sly and devious.

**Sheridan, Richard Brinsley** (1751–1816) Famous playwright and close companion of George and Charles James Fox. Also an MP and famous for his speech on the impeachment of Warren Hastings. A great *bon viveur* – whose red nose was made famous by the caricaturists. Politically he and the Whigs drifted away from George who saw little of him after 1812. He died in poverty.

**Smith, Sydney** (1771–1845) The most celebrated wit of his day. A polemicist for Whig causes but Grey rewarded him with just a canonry at St Paul's in 1830.

**Sophia, Princess** (1777–1848) Fifth daughter of George III. Unmarried, she had an illegitimate daughter and old General Garth was declared the father. However, many thought the real father was her brother, the Duke of Cumberland.

**Sussex, Duke of** (1773–1843) 6th son of George III. He lived abroad until 1804 and was a patron of the arts and sciences. No heir.

**Talleyrand, Charles Maurice de** (1754–1838) A great survivor. Bishop of Autun under the Ancien Regime, he survived the guillotine by being in England 1792–94. Foreign Minister under the Directory and then under Napoleon 1797–1807. Disgraced in 1809 but Foreign Minister again under Louis XVIII 1814–15. Became ambassador to London under Louis-Philippe 1830–34.

**Wellington, The Duke of** (1769–1852) Built his reputation in India. He beat the Napoleonic armies in the Peninsular campaign 1808–13 and Napoleon himself at Waterloo. He was a Tory Cabinet minister 1818–27, Prime Minister 1828–30 and briefly again for a month in 1834. Leader of the Lords in Peel's Government of 1841–46.

**Weltje, Louis** (1745–1810) A German who started as a gingerbread-baker and became George's cook and companion. He dabbled in property and found George's first house in Brighton.

**Wyatville, Sir Jeffry** (1766–1840) A nephew of the architect James Wyatt. Architect at Windsor Castle from 1824; knighted in 1828, at which point he changed his surname.

**Yarmouth, The Earl of** (1777–1842) His mother – Lady Hertford – was a mistress of George. He became 3rd Marquis of Hertford in 1822. Like George, a close friend, he was a great collector who amassed most of the Wallace Collection. His unsavoury reputation made him the model for the Marquis of Steyne in Thackeray's *Vanity Fair* and Lord Monmouth in Disraeli's *Coningsby*.

**York, The Duke of** (1763–1827) The second son of George III. Commanded the British troops in Flanders, 1793–95. Commander-in-Chief 1798–1809. Resigned because his mistress trafficked in military titles. Re-instated 1811. An inveterate gambler, he was usually in debt. Commemorated by the statue at the top of the Duke of York steps, Waterloo Place, London. The closest of the family to George.

# Chronology

**1762** *12 August*. George Augustus Frederick born at St James's Palace. Given the title of Prince of Wales at his birth

**1772** George III introduced the Royal Marriages Act to forbid the marriage of any descendant of George II under the age of twenty-five without royal permission

**1779** George starts his first 'public' affair with the actress Mary Robinson
George establishes a friendship with Charles James Fox

**1780** A separate establishment is provided for George on his eighteenth birthday

**1781** The British army surrenders at Yorktown

**1782** Lord North resigns as Prime Minister

**1783** Carlton House given to George by his father and Henry Holland appointed to rebuild it
George receives a civil allowance of £50,000 from the Civil List
Fox–North coalition
*December*. George III dismisses the coalition and appoints William Pitt as Prime Minister

**1784** George falls in love with Maria Fitzherbert
Pitt wins the general election

**1785** *15 December*. George and Maria 'married' in London

**1786** *July*. As a measure of retrenchment, George takes Maria and his circle of friends to Brighton and rents a farmhouse close to the sea

**1788** *October*. George III succumbs to his first bout of madness – leads to the Regency Crisis

**1789** *23 February*. The King recovers
*14 July*. Outbreak of the French Revolution

**1793** Execution of Louis XVI. War declared against France

**1794** George starts his relationship with Lady Jersey

**1795** *8 April*. George marries Princess Caroline of Brunswick

**1796** *7 January*. Birth of Princess Charlotte

**1799** Maria Fitzherbert returns to favour

**1801** Ireland united to Britain to form the United Kingdom
George III dismisses Pitt over Catholic emancipation
Addington becomes Prime Minister
George III ill

**1802** Peace of Amiens between Britain and France

**1803** War with France resumed

**1804** George III again falls ill for five months
Pitt returns as Prime Minister
George is reconciled with his father

**1805** *October*. Nelson's victory at Trafalgar

**1806** Pitt dies, succeeded by Lord Grenville as Prime Minister, who forms a coalition: 'The Ministry of All the Talents'
Fox becomes Foreign Secretary but dies in September
The 'Delicate Investigation' into Caroline's conduct at Blackheath
George starts his relationship with Lady Hertford

**1807** Government dismissed over Catholic emancipation

**1808** Beginning of the Peninsular War

**1809** The Duke of York forced to resign as Commander-in-Chief
Spencer Perceval becomes Prime Minister

**1810** George III relapses into his final illness

**1811** *6 February*. George becomes Regent
George ends his relationship with Maria Fitzherbert

**1812** Restrictions on the Regent removed
Perceval assassinated. Liverpool appointed Prime Minister

**1813** Nash commissioned to redesign the Brighton Pavilion and to start the grand design for central London

**1815** Napoleon defeated at Waterloo

**1816** Princess Charlotte marries Prince Leopold of Saxe-Coburg-Saalfeld

**1817** Princess Charlotte dies after giving birth to a stillborn son

**1818** Queen Charlotte dies

**1819** Princess Victoria born. Her father is Edward, Duke of Kent
Peterloo Massacre in Manchester

**1820** *29 January*. George III dies. Accession of George IV
Lady Conyngham becomes the royal favourite
*June*. Caroline returns to England
*August*. Caroline's trial starts
*November*. Bill of Pains and Penalties dropped

**1821** *5 May*. Napoleon dies
*19 July*. Coronation of George IV
*7 August*. Caroline dies
Royal Progress to Ireland

**1822** Royal Progress to Scotland

**1823** Canning joins Government as Foreign Secretary

**1827** *April*. Canning replaces Liverpool as Prime Minister
Canning dies. Goderich becomes Prime Minister

**1828** Wellington becomes Prime Minister
*July*. Daniel O'Connell wins the Clare by-election

**1829** *April*. Catholic Relief Act

**1830** *26 June*. George dies

## The County Fire Office and the Quadrant

As a speculative venture, John Nash built a majestic sweeping façade of two continuous Doric colonnades in front of the buildings in Regent Street. This experiment in covered shopping was ahead of its time, for by 1848 the shopkepers had found their shops to be too small, dark and poky, and the colonnades were removed. Later that century, Nash's stucco buildings gave way to those faced with Portland stone and two Nash churches in Regent Street were torn down in 1904.

# Further Reading

Adams, M., *A Parody on the Political House that Jack Built,* London, 1820

Adolphus, J. H. (ed.), *The Trial of Her Majesty Caroline,* London, 1820

—, *The Last Days, Death, Funeral Obsequies of Her Late Majesty Caroline,* London, 1822

Anon, *The Free-born Englishman,* London, 1820

—, *The Queen and her Powers,* London, 1820

—, *The Queen of Trumps,* London, 1820

Aspinall, Arthur, *Politics and the Press 1780–1850,* 1949

— (ed.), *The Letters of King George IV,* 3 vols, Cambridge, 1938

— (ed.), *The Correspondence of George, Prince of Wales,* 8 vols, London, 1963–71

Ayling, Stanley, *Fox,* London, 1991

Bamford, Francis (ed.), *The Journal of Mrs Arbuthnot,* 2 vols, London, 1950

Byrne, Paula, *Perdita: The Life of Mary Robinson,* London, 2004

*Carlton House: The Past Glories of George IV's Palace,* exh.cat.,The Queen's Gallery, Buckingham Palace, London, 1991

Chambers, James, *Palmerston, the People's Darling,* London, 2004

Creevey, Thomas, *The Creevey Papers,* London, 1963

Croker, John Wilson, *The Croker Papers,* London, 1884

Croly, George, *The Life and Times of His Late Majesty George the Fourth,* London, 1830

David, Saul, *Prince of Pleasure: The Prince of Wales and the Making of the Regency,* London and New York, 1998

Donald, Diana, *The Age of Caricature,* New Haven and London, 1996

Ehrman, J., *The Younger Pitt,* 3 vols, London, 1969–96

Fraser, Flora, *The Unruly Queen: The Life of Queen Caroline,* London, 1996

Gash, Norman, *Lord Liverpool,* London, 1984

George, Dorothy, *Catalogue of Political and Personal Satires Preserved in the Department of Prints and Drawings in the British Museum,* vols 6–10, London, 1938–52

—, *English Political Caricature,* 2 vols, Oxford, 1959

*George IV in Edinburgh 1822,* exh. cat., Scottish National Portrait Gallery, Edinburgh, 1961

Greville, Charles, *The Greville Memoirs 1814–1860,* 7 vols, London, 1938

Hamilton, Anne, *The Authentic Records of the Court of England for the Last Seventy Years,* London, 1832

Hibbert, Christopher, *George IV,* 2 vols, London, 1972 & 1973

Hill, Draper, *Mr Gillray: The Caricaturist,* London, 1965

Hinde, Wendy, *George Canning,* London, 1973

Hobhouse, Christopher, *Fox,* London, 1934

Hone, William, *The Political House that Jack Built,* London, 1819

—, *Non mi ricordo!,* London, 1820

—, *The Queen's Matrimonial Ladder,* London, 1820

Hughes-Hallett, Penelope, *The Immortal Dinner,* London, 2000

Huish, Robert, *An Authentic History of the Coronation of His Majesty King George the Fourth,* London, 1821

—, *Memoirs of George the Fourth,* London, 1831

Jones, Clyve, and David Lewis Jones, *Peers, Politics and Power: The House of Lords 1603–1911,* London, 1986

Krumbhaar, E. B., *Isaac Cruikshank,* Philadelphia, 1966

Longford, Elizabeth, *Wellington: The Years of the Sword,* London, 1969

—, *Wellington: Pillar of State,* London, 1972

Munson, James, *Maria Fitzherbert, the Secret Wife of George IV,* London, 2001

Murray, Venetia, *High Society: A Social History of the Regency Period, 1788–1830,* London, 1998

Olsen, D. J., *Town Planning in London,* New Haven and London, 1964

Parissien, Steven, *Regency Style,* London, 1992

—, *George IV: The Grand Entertainment,* London, 2001

Patten, Robert L., *George Cruikshank's Life, Times and Art,* vol. 1, 1792–1835, London, 1992

Peakman, Julie, *Mighty Lewd Books,* Basingstoke, 2003

Plumb, J. H., *The First Four Georges,* London, 1956

Prebble, John, *The King's Jaunt: George IV in Scotland, August 1822,* London, 1988

Priestley, J. B., *The Prince of Pleasure and his Regency,* London, 1969

Roberts, Jane (ed.), *Royal Treasures: A Golden Jubilee Celebration,* London, 2002

Röhl, J. C. G., Martin Warren and David Hunt, *The Purple Secret: Genes, Madness and the Royal Houses of Europe,* London, 1998

Rolo, P. J. V., *George Canning,* London, 1965

Smith, E. A., *George IV,* New Haven and London, 1999

Stourton, Lord, *Memoirs of Mrs Fitzherbert,* 1856

Summerson, John, *The Life and Work of John Nash,* London, 1980

—, *Georgian London,* rev. edn., London, 1988

Thackeray, W. M., *The Four Georges,* London, 1855

Tomalin, Claire, *Mrs Jordan's Profession,* London and New York, 1994

Turberville, A. S., *The House of Lords in the Age of Reform, 1784–1837,* London, 1958

Wardroper, John, *Kings, Lords and Wicked Libellers: Satire and Protest, 1760–1837,* London, 1973

—, *The Caricatures of George Cruikshank,* London, 1977

—, *Wicked Ernest,* London, 2002

Wilkins, W. H., *Mrs Fitzherbert and George IV,* London, 1905 (first publication of the proof of marriage)

Wilson, Frances, *The Courtesan's Revenge: Harriette Wilson, the Woman who Blackmailed the King,* London, 2003

Wilson, Harriette, *Memoirs,* 4 vols, London, 1825

Ziegler, Philip, *Addington,* London, 1965

## Nash's London – his 'Metropolitan Improvements' from Regents Park to Charing Cross

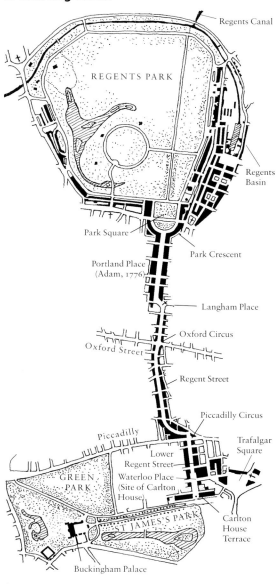

This scheme stretched from the cutting of the Regents Canal to serve the Regents Basin, to reconstruction of the west end of the Strand and the creation of what was to become Trafalgar Square. It provided a spine for London's West End. Crabb Robinson said that Regents Park and Regent Street 'will give a sort of glory to the Regent's Government which will be more felt by remote posterity than the victories of Trafalgar and Waterloo, glorious as they are.'

# Index